Model Music Programs

Ideas for Everyone

MICHAEL BLAKESLEE, LINDA C. BROWN,
AND ASHLEY OPP HOFMANN

MENC The National Association for
MUSIC EDUCATION
1907 - 2007

Published in partnership with
MENC: The National Association for Music Education
Frances S. Ponick, Executive Editor

ROWMAN & LITTLEFIELD EDUCATION
Lanham • New York • Toronto • Plymouth, UK

Published in partnership with
MENC: The National Association for Music Education

Published in the United States of America
by Rowman & Littlefield Education
A Division of Rowman & Littlefield Publishers, Inc.
A wholly owned subsidiary of The Rowman & Littlefield Publishing Group, Inc.
4501 Forbes Boulevard, Suite 200, Lanham, Maryland 20706
www.rowmaneducation.com

Estover Road
Plymouth PL6 7PY
United Kingdom

British Library Cataloguing in Publication Information Available

Library of Congress Cataloging-in-Publication Data

Blakeslee, Michael.
  Model music programs : ideas for everyone / Michael Blakeslee, Linda C. Brown, and
Ashley Opp Hofmann.
    p. cm.
  ISBN-13: 978-1-57886-729-5 (cloth : alk. paper)
  ISBN-13: 978-1-57886-730-1 (pbk. : alk. paper)
  ISBN-10: 1-57886-729-0 (cloth : alk. paper)
  ISBN-10: 1-57886-730-4 (pbk. : alk. paper)
  1. School music—Instruction and study—United States—Case studies. I. Brown,
Linda C. II. Hofmann, Ashley Opp. III. MENC, the National Association for Music
Education (U.S.) IV. Title.
  MT3.U5B63 2007
  780.71'073—dc22   2007035986

∞™ The paper used in this publication meets the minimum requirements of American
National Standard for Information Sciences—Permanence of Paper for Printed Library
Materials, ANSI/NISO Z39.48-1992.
Manufactured in the United States of America

Contents

Foreword

What is a Model Music Program? Is it the music course with innovative curriculum? Perhaps this type of course or courses is "model" because of a motivational instructor? Could this program simply be a solid series of offerings within a community that truly supports the arts? Maybe it is laced with brand-new, outside-the-box ideas?

The chapters and examples in this book show a diverse variety of music programs throughout the country that have touched students and communities. These programs are from many different socioeconomic areas and include all sizes of communities, from the largest urban areas to the tiniest rural places in the United States. Some of these exemplary music programs are driven by one energetic teacher, others are guided by an entire music staff, and still others are jump-started by visionary administrators. No matter where one teaches, there can exist a Model Music Program.

MENC: The National Association for Music Education has long recognized and promoted excellent instruction and innovative solutions to the challenges of teaching a core subject that doesn't quite fit the average academic mold—thank goodness! This book seeks to inspire and encourage good teachers to take their music programs to the next level. The following pages describe how to make a music program in any setting a model for good teaching. In addition, this book is full of success stories—they demonstrate that in some cases success can come from the most meager beginnings.

As you read about the Model Music Programs, realize that you already have the tools to build your own model program. Let us know about your progress and your own program. May this book be the first of many volumes of Model Music Programs!

Renee Westlake, Music Supervisor
Bozeman Public Schools
Bozeman, Montana

Acknowledgment

The contents of this publication were developed under a grant from the U.S. Department of Education. However, the contents do not necessarily represent the policy of the Department of Education, and you should not assume endorsement by the federal government.

Introduction

What This Book Is About

In 2004, MENC: The National Association for Music Education launched a nationwide search for Model Music Programs, not necessarily "perfect" programs, but admirable programs that offered replicable ways of organizing and maintaining high-quality music education in accordance with MENC's mission to provide music education for all students. Begun as a grassroots campaign by MENC members in Pennsylvania, Washington, and many other states and funded by a U.S. Department of Education grant, the project, titled "Music for All: Building a Training and Support System for Music Teachers to Better Serve American Youth," solicited all types of music programs. Bands, orchestras, choirs, and general music classes, elementary to secondary, underfunded to highly funded—all were invited to submit descriptions of their programs. Of particular interest were urban music programs, rural music programs, and programs found in economically disadvantaged areas because successful music educators and administrators working there often excel at creative management of few resources.

Music educators and administrators around the country responded with information about their resources, scheduling, facilities, and community and booster club support, as well as budget and school administration support. Participants provided lesson plans or other materials that adhered to the nine National Standards for Music Education. No program was too large or too small, but under the terms of the grant, only twelve could be chosen to receive special recognition, which included $1,500 in support of each of the programs and participation in a panel discussion at the MENC National Conference in Salt Lake City in April 2006.

Seeking models that demonstrated best practices, innovative ideas, good use of resources, and a solid foundation in the National Standards for Music Education, representatives of the music education profession reviewed the submissions of their educator colleagues. This committee, which consisted of three MENC member educators, agreed to tackle all 156 profiles of high-achieving music programs that came from schools and districts in 45 states. The program judges were Nancy Ditmer, professor of music education at The College of Wooster and past president of the North Central Division of MENC; Aurelia Hartenberger, curriculum director of Mehlville School District, St. Louis, and adjunct associate professor of music at the University of Missouri, St. Louis, and past president of the Southwest Division of MENC; and Renee Westlake, music supervisor for the Bozeman, Montana, Public Schools and past president of the Northwest Division of MENC. Because of the amazing variety of successful programs submitted, the judges' task was far more difficult than anyone expected. All concurred with Renee Westlake, who said "it was impressive to discover what a wide variety of excellent music programs this country has at all levels, from traditional ones to those molded to fit a unique population."

Because the terms of the grant restricted them from choosing more than twelve programs, the judges reluctantly agreed to that limitation and got to work. In addition to selecting the twelve, they nominated two additional programs for honorable mention and insisted that the valuable contributions of the remaining entries not be ignored.

The chapters that follow describe the twelve selected music education programs in terms of four categories: technology, interdisciplinary and multicultural learning, music for all, and standards-based learning. Obviously built through the hard work and investment of the music educators and administrators, many of the other programs overcame numerous obstacles to achieve success. Including as much information as possible about these music programs was a no-brainer. They are discussed in chapters 1–4, and a list of all participating schools and districts can be found in appendix B.

By showcasing these music education programs, MENC hopes to share their successes and techniques with all music educators. These programs provide models for building and maintaining exemplary music programs in the future. In addition, this book also provides resources and ideas for assisting music educators in various facets of their work with students, administrators, and the community. Most of the resources listed in the following pages are available without cost and can be found either on the MENC website or at libraries. Librarians can show readers how to obtain material from MENC magazines and journals using database information services.

While the study of models has been a tradition for music educators, we have plucked key elements from the music programs for the broader music education community. We invite you to replicate, modify, and adopt them in your schools and districts across the country. As you read through the ideas and resources presented here, we hope you will find inspiration, information, and support in our common quest—to provide quality music education for all.

Many of the resources provided in this book can be found on the Internet. While we have made every effort to facilitate finding the information you need, Web addresses do frequently change. If you find that a Web address we've listed is no longer valid, try searching the organization's website for the information or try using a search engine to find a link to the term, person, organization, or phrase you're after.

1

Technology

It has become almost cliché to describe how quickly technology and education change, but new technologies change music education daily, pushing educators to explore ways that students can experience, create, and enjoy music. Simultaneously, working with technology prepares students to compete more competently in an increasingly global and competitive society.

When it comes to technology, students are often ahead of their teachers. They already play with and use the latest forms of media outside of the school day. Yet model classrooms and pedagogy are not state of the art for the sake of being state of the art; these programs conscientiously use technology in ways that contribute to learning. Successful music teachers in model programs integrate technology into a carefully planned curriculum.

The following programs—South Eastern School District, Haley Elementary School, and East Ramapo Central School District—use technology in myriad ways. Technology plays vastly different roles in each of these music programs, including the way in which programs use it and the degree to which classrooms adopt it.

SOUTH EASTERN SCHOOL DISTRICT

Basic School Description

South Eastern School District in Fawn Grove, Pennsylvania, serves 3,281 students. Primarily rural, the district draws from a geographically large area in

York County, Pennsylvania. Six schools comprise the district: three elementary schools located in or near small towns (Delta-Peach Bottom, Fawn Area, Stewartstown), a building for grades 5–6 (South Eastern Middle School West), another building for grades 7–8 (South Eastern Middle School East), and a high school for grades 9–12 (Kennard-Dale). The district has 242 teachers, and the total pupil-to-teacher ratio is 13.5 to 1. Carl Barr, the Fine Arts Department leader at Kennard-Dale High School, submitted South Eastern School District. The district's total per-pupil expenditure is $5,479.

Budget and Other Funding

For general materials, the elementary schools budget approximately $2,800 annually, and middle schools receive $4,500. The category of "general materials" excludes textbooks and recordings and instrument purchase or repair, for which a districtwide instrument fund for purchase, replacement, and repair provides approximately $12,000 per year.

The total high school music budget is $26,000 per year. Of this budget, $6,000 is directed to music and general supplies, while $20,000 goes toward student activities. This figure excludes salaries, extracurricular contract pay (which consists of eleven positions ranging from $900 to $3,800 each), instrument purchase and replacement, textbooks, recordings, and major uniform purchases. The district purchased new marching band uniforms in April 2006. All major textbook and recording resources are purchased from district-wide curriculum funds.

The PTO/PTA in the elementary schools occasionally provides money for supplementary materials. The Kennard-Dale Music Boosters Association (for the high school and middle school) provides money for ongoing expenses like concert receptions, supplemental field trips, the marching band banquet, and the senior awards banquet. The boosters hold special fundraisers for the uniform fund. For example, $22,000 was spent for choral gowns and ensemble outfits in fall 2003.

Scheduling

Elementary students in grades 1–4 have two forty-minute music classes per six-day cycle for the entire year. Kindergarteners receive one twenty-minute music class per six-day cycle. Band and orchestra lessons begin in fourth grade, with one thirty-minute group pull-out lesson per cycle.

All students in grades 5 and 6 receive one music class per six-day cycle. Students in grades 7 and 8 participate in music classes every day for a quarter. All middle school students (grades 5–8) also have the opportunity to participate in chorus, band, and orchestra, as well as group instrument lessons.

At the high school level, a variety of music classes and major performing ensembles meets during the school day, three times per cycle all year, with ensembles receiving priority scheduling. Students can participate in both vocal and instrumental music if they choose. The school maintains a one-credit fine arts requirement for graduation; music classes can satisfy this requirement or requirements for other elective credits. Most music courses are open to all students without previous experience or prerequisites. Students may elect music technology courses, which also meet the school's one-credit technology requirement for graduation.

Kennard-Dale High School maintains three choirs designed to maximize student development in singing. Students audition for the concert choir (sixty-five to seventy singers), which is comprised of mostly eleventh and twelfth graders and a few outstanding sophomores. Chorus (eighty to one hundred singers) is a mixed-voice group open to students in grades 10–12, as well as male singers in grade 9 and male singers from the concert choir. A third choir, the treble choir (fifty to sixty-five singers), is open to female singers in ninth grade and female singers from the concert choir. Students from the concert choir who participate in the chorus and treble choir serve as models in demonstrating good vocal technique for the younger, less-experienced singers.

Small vocal groups, such as vocal ensemble, men's quartet, and K-Dettes (ten female voices), rehearse before school, and a string ensemble, brass quintet, jazz band, and pep band all rehearse before or after school. These groups perform for community groups, such as senior centers, elementary schools, churches, and community and school events.

Music Facilities and Equipment

All music classrooms have a stereo and a piano or Clavinova, along with texts, recordings, and other resources to deliver curriculum. Each school has a centralized music room equipped with a computer, MIDI keyboard, printer, and tape deck on a cart. Music stations are furnished with notation, sequencing, and theory software, as well as software that corresponds with the current music series for each school. The district continually examines the music curriculum and plans for technology upgrades.

All schools have a piano or Clavinova for rehearsal and instruction, as well as music stands, music chairs, and a music library. For band, schools have larger woodwind and brass instruments and a range of percussion instruments (a full complement in the high school, timpani and most percussion in the upper middle school, and basic percussion in the lower middle and elementary schools). For orchestra, cellos and basses are available as needed districtwide. The district also rents available string instruments for $25 per year so students are not excluded for financial reasons. The district purchased some of these, and others were donated. Larger instruments are made available in school because they are difficult to transport between home and school. For the choral program, grand pianos are available in the high school rehearsal room and auditorium and the upper middle school auditorium.

Since being recognized as a model program, the district upgraded the equipment in the high school music technology lab and transferred the previous equipment to the upper middle school. Students at the middle level will use the equipment primarily for keyboard instruction, music theory, and instrument study units.

Philosophy of Music Education

South Eastern School District believes that music instruction constitutes an essential part of student learning and growth. The district maintains a strong music curriculum that undergoes major review every six years, and revision and expansion occur as needed and as approved by the Curriculum Council, administrators, and school board. All music classes and groups that meet during school time have a planned course of study. Through effective instruction and the use of appropriate content, materials, and assessments, all students are encouraged to reach their greatest potential in music and to meet national and state standards in music and the arts. High school students must meet a one-credit fine arts requirement for graduation.

Unique Aspects of the Program

South Eastern School District considers providing exciting, hands-on music instruction for all students—even at the high school level—its greatest "unique" strength.

The music technology program at the high school has grown from one section of 27 students when the lab first opened six years ago to twelve sections at three levels and serving about 230 students currently. The courses—Music Technology I, II, and III—are open to all students in the school for hands-on music instruction with keyboards and computers using accompaniment, sequencing, notation, audio recording, and editing software.

In Music Technology I, students learn to play, improvise, compose, arrange, and create music using computers, MIDI keyboards, and selected software. In Music Technology II, students extend their skills to include audio recording, mixing MIDI and live audio, video recording, and combined video and audio recording. In Music Technology III, projects focus on students' interests in composition, audio recording, editing, and video/audio recording and editing.

Regardless of musical background or ability level, special needs students and gifted students alike have the opportunity to be successful musically and creatively. Given the hands-on and creative nature of the music technology program, students who cared little for music have become excited about it,

Music technology students at Kennard-Dale High School in South Eastern School District enjoy hands-on learning by arranging and creating music.

and many have become more involved in other areas of music and music performance.

Kennard-Dale High School also includes innovative courses, such as Survey of the Fine Arts, a hands-on historical arts instruction program taught jointly by a music and an art teacher. American Music I examines the vocal, choral, and piano music of America, while American Music II focuses on band and orchestral music. Both American Music I and II highlight composers and performers of Pennsylvania. A course titled Folk/Country/Jazz/Rock explores the history of contemporary popular music. During the school day, Kennard-Dale maintains three choirs, one band, and one orchestra and provides Voice Training and Music Theory/Ear Training courses.

Beginning in the summer of 2003, the school district began funding summer band lessons and rehearsals for elementary and middle school students. During this six-week program, students participate one morning per week for three hours for like-instrument group lessons and a large group rehearsal. School music staff and local certified instructors teach the program, assisted by high school students. At the conclusion of the six-week period, students perform for family and friends. Students pay a minimal fee for participation in the program.

Latest Developments

Since submitting the district's music program as an MENC: The National Association for Music Education Model Music Program, South Eastern has increased its use of music technology in the music classroom. The district is in the process of securing a Yamaha MIE lab and program for the fifth- and sixth-grade building as part of curricular instruction. A grant received from the York County Alliance for Learning has been used to purchase additional audio editing software for the high school music technology lab. The district is also proposing to incorporate more Orff instruction in the elementary schools and world drumming in the middle schools. Some of the money South Eastern received for its recognition as a Model Music Program has been allotted for curricular materials and will be used to purchase additional instruments. Finally, the district proposes adding the following two new courses for the high school next year: an advanced placement (AP) music theory course and a technology course dealing with sound, lighting, and recording techniques used for musical productions and concerts.

HALEY ELEMENTARY SCHOOL, FORT WAYNE COMMUNITY SCHOOLS

Basic School Description

Located in Fort Wayne, Indiana, and part of the Fort Wayne School District, Haley Elementary School is an urban school with a student population of 604 (2006–2007). Music teacher Wendy Bloom submitted Haley Elementary School to the Model Music Program. All students at Haley participate in music classes. The per-pupil expenditure is $7,470.

Budget and Other Funding

Approximately $300–$400 is budgeted for music annually, with the school's PTA supplementing funding for special programs and cultural events. Since the initial grant application, the school system has implemented a $1 per student funding amount for music and other special area subjects, increasing the annual school music budget to approximately $600. Grants and awards, initiated by the music teacher, provide additional funding, and amounts vary. The school's technology committee periodically replaces hardware and software for the program's music technology lab, with funding amounts ranging from approximately $800–$3,000. Last year, the program's music technology lab was upgraded with approximately $6,000 in funding from the school's capital project funds. Donations collected from musical programs total $200 or less annually.

Scheduling

Students in grades 1–5 have two thirty-minute general music classes each week that include recorder instruction in the fourth grade. Kindergarteners have one thirty-minute music class each week. The Haley Elementary School Choir has one forty-five-minute class period per week, scheduled during the school day. Various after-school music ensembles and activities take place from 3:30–5:00. These include the Indiana Music Educators–sponsored Circle the State with Song Ensemble (sixteen to twenty fifth-grade students rehearse weekly October to February), Haley Indiana All-State Honors Choir (one to five students rehearse as needed December to January), Haley Elementary School Chimers (nine to twelve fourth- and fifth-grade students rehearse weekly), and the Haley Elementary School Drum Circle (nine to twelve fourth- and fifth-grade students practice once weekly, February to May).

Additional music opportunities include K–5 Musical Characters (twelve to twenty-four students), who rehearse twice per week for four to six weeks during the school year, and the Foundation for Art and Music in Elementary Education/Fort Wayne Philharmonic Composition Project, where two fourth-grade students participate in three to four music composition sessions with a composer-in-residence and rehearse and perform a completed composition with the Philharmonic. Two to five students take part in the Haley Elementary School Indiana State School Music Association Piano Solo and Ensemble Contest, with scheduled rehearsals as necessary.

Music Facilities and Equipment

The Haley Music Department facilitates an Indiana Department of Education Technology Enriched Model Classroom with a networked multiworkstation music technology lab. It includes a SmartBoard (an interactive, electronic whiteboard), an LCD display projector, and print center. With some manipulation, the room accommodates an Orff instrumentarium with pitched and unpitched percussion instruments, floor space for movement activities, risers for singing, an acoustic piano, a CD player, a VCR/TV, and music textbook carts. Shelving areas and a storage closet occupy part of the room as well.

In the music technology lab, students use fifteen Internet-connected workstations that include eMac ("education Mac") and new iMac computers and Yamaha PSR 292 electronic keyboards with interfaces, foot pedals, earphones, and splitter cables. Students use various music instruction, notation, and sequencing software programs as well as various multimedia programs within an upgraded Mac operating system. Additionally, students use network folders for saving files and interact regularly with a music website and weblog site.

The lab includes a teacher music technology workstation equipped with a laptop, electronic piano keyboard, LCD projector, SmartBoard, and document camera. Other teacher hardware and software include an external hard drive, handheld PDA with keyboard, several iPods, external speakers, digital recorder, digital camcorder with various microphones and tripod, digital camera, and various music and multimedia software programs. The teacher also has access to one of several Tandberg units to enable videoconferencing. The school system's elementary music teachers share sixty guitars, thirty ukuleles, and one set of digital wind, string, and drum controllers.

Philosophy of Music Education

Fort Wayne Community Schools hold the philosophy that music education is an integral part of educating the whole child. The school district considers music part of the core curriculum for grades K–5, and students receive graded instruction and evaluation in general music, choral, instrumental, and other appropriate music-related classes. Additionally, the school system favors integration of music instruction as a part of each school's school improvement plan (SIP) to support student achievement in math, language arts, social studies, and science.

The Haley music curriculum is aligned with the Indiana Academic Standards for Music as well as with the National Standards for Music Education. Student assessment and grade report cards are correlated with the Indiana Academic Standards for Music.

Unique Aspects of the Program

At Haley Elementary School, students participate in a musical education in a "standard-embedded, technology-enriched" learning environment. All music lessons, projects, and activities integrate technology in one form or another. Setting up the classroom and pedagogy within a constructivist theoretical framework, the Haley music program encourages students to work collaboratively on projects that use both Schulwerk and Kodály methodologies and technology-driven assessment. State-of-the-art educational technologies permit students to learn in an interactive environment that is also aligned with standards for music technology, music education, educational technology, and Indiana's State Music Academic Standards.

The Haley music program aims to connect the related arts of music, art, and dance to language arts, social studies, and math.

Haley Elementary School's music classroom is an Indiana Department of Education Technology-Enriched Model Classroom. In conjunction with the district's participation in the state's Technology Professional Development Program, the music teacher applied for and received a $30,000 grant. The classroom is a multiworkstation music technology lab that includes electronic keyboards, music software, digital instruments, MIDI, and various multimedia tools. Students participate in a completely interactive curriculum aligned with computer-assisted instruction lessons and piano instruction. They compose digital music compositions, pursue various Web research projects, and create multimedia

Fourth-grade students at Haley Elementary School explore their "musical signature" compositions using the program's music technology lab.

presentations. With the use of technology, student assessments, such as music portfolios, are now part of the school network folders in various media formats.

In 2003, fifth-grade students used music technologies for a world music project that studied African music and culture. The Music Department received a $28,000 grant from the Indiana Department of Education in conjunction with the project. Students integrated music technology, multimedia, and various learning technologies as they accessed a WebQuest site titled *Capture the Heart Beat of . . . Africa!* to explore various African cultural arts websites. In addition, they used digital forms of photography, video, audio, and music sequencing and notation software to create and communicate Web presentations that focused on African percussion.

Latest Developments

Haley's music program continues to integrate technology and music. In March 2006, Haley Elementary School hosted Titos Sompa and the Mbongi

Dance Theater for an interactive assembly that focused on African music and culture. In collaboration with the district's Technology Department and ACELINK at Indiana Purdue University in Fort Wayne, the program was videoconferenced to students at three additional, remote schools in the district. Haley's music program received a National Education Foundation Grant to further extend the project.

As part of MENC's National Anthem Project, Haley students integrated music, art, language arts, and social studies as they accessed the Smithsonian's Museum of American History website. They learned about the historical and cultural origins of "The Star-Spangled Banner" as they rehearsed, memorized, and prepared to perform the national anthem during the September 2006 Star-Spangled Banner Day.

In November 2006, Haley hosted the 2006–2007 FAME/Fort Wayne Philharmonic Composition Project, where twenty-five northeastern Indiana fourth-grade student composers met with Composer-in-Residence David Crowe to explore various African American art forms to collaborate on creating an original orchestral jazz composition to be performed by the Fort Wayne Philharmonic.

EAST RAMAPO CENTRAL SCHOOL DISTRICT

Basic District Description

East Ramapo Central School District in Spring Valley, New York, has ten elementary schools, five of which are K–3 and five are 4–6: Colton, Eldorado, Elmwood, Fleetwood, Grandview, Hempstead, Hillcrest, Lime Kiln, Margetts, and Summit Park. The district has two middle schools for grades 7–8: Chestnut Ridge and Pomona. There are two high schools: Spring Valley and Ramapo High School. Ramapo High School's ninth graders attend the Ramapo Freshman Center. Ramapo Central School District is suburban and has a total school population of 8,946, with a pupil-to-teacher ratio of 11 to 1. Schools in this district have a total of thirty-three music teachers. Gail Calisoff, supervisor of music and art, submitted East Ramapo Central School District to the Model Music Program competition. East Ramapo's total per-pupil expenditure is $19,046.

Budget and Other Funding

The district budgets $53,500 for elementary school music supplies and materials as well as instruments, instrument rental and repairs, and participation in the New York State School Music Association and county festivals. The middle schools and high schools share a budget of $52,000 for supplies and materials that is distributed among band, chorus, orchestra, and general music. The high schools also receive $37,315 for the marching band.

State Senator Thomas Morahan's office gave the district an $8,000 grant for the marching band. Marching band parents raise funds by doing coin drops, and they recently hosted a U.S. Scholastic Band Association Marching Band Festival. Parents support their children's band programs in specific ways as requested by the band director, such as performing quartermaster duties and chaperoning.

Scheduling

In the elementary schools, students in grades 1–3 participate in forty minutes per week of general music, which includes playing the recorder. Third graders also take part in an additional forty-minute chorus rehearsal each week.

Students in grades 4–6 have general music forty minutes per week. In addition to general music, students elect to take band, orchestra, and chorus. Students may participate in band and chorus or orchestra and chorus. The performing groups rehearse once a week during recess, and each instrumental student receives a forty-minute instrumental lesson weekly.

East Ramapo's middle school students have an A/B schedule, where classes meet every other day. They choose from electives such as Concert Band I, Concert Band II, Beginning Band, Orchestra, Junior Orchestra, and Beginning Orchestra. General music classes consist of Keyboard/Computers. In the middle schools, every student who does not participate in a performing group takes Keyboard/Computer. This class goes throughout the year.

The two high schools in East Ramapo Central School District have Band, Orchestra, and General Music everyday for twenty weeks. They also take Keyboard/Computers, though it lasts only half of the school year. High school students in performing groups rehearse each day for forty minutes. Though it is difficult for students to participate in more than one group, students may "share" groups if rehearsals take place during the same period by splitting their time in each.

Music Facilities and Equipment

Elementary music classrooms have a piano, full Orff instruments, and rhythm instruments. Each classroom has a computer and keyboard with Sibelius, Music Ace, and Cakewalk installed.

Band classrooms have stands, chairs, music, and a full complement of in-struments. Orchestra programs have stands, chairs, music, and large instru-ments. Band and orchestra rooms also have ten computers and twenty PSR-Yamaha keyboards. The choral classrooms have built-in risers, a piano, and a music library.

The district pays the rental fees of instruments for all students who receive free or reduced lunch and who wish to be a part of the music program.

Each middle school and high school has a music lab that contains ten com-puters and twenty keyboards. Students use the labs to learn how to play the keyboard. Using the Sonar and Sibelius Music Ace program, they are able to both compose and perform their compositions. Both special education stu-dents and regular education students use the labs.

Philosophy of Music Education

The East Ramapo Central School District is committed to providing every student with an opportunity to study music. The district aims to edu-cate the whole child and recognizes that a comprehensive education for a whole human being means offering a musical opportunity for each student to deeply explore his or her individual potential. All music instruction in-cludes the New York State Learning Standards for the Arts as well as the Na-tional Standards.

The district holds the belief that a Model Music Program begins with the individual educator and his or her commitment to excellence. Music teachers in East Ramapo focus on preparing students to be musicians in their future lives, regardless of what profession they choose.

Unique Aspects of the Program

The East Ramapo Central School District describes itself as a multicul-tural district. Like many school districts, the student body is composed of diverse students from all backgrounds and levels of incomes working to-gether each day.

East Ramapo has a remarkably strong instrumental program, beginning in the fourth grade. The music programs have strong interdisciplinary links to all academic subjects. For example, teachers link the music program to literacy through score writing. Cultural lessons add another dimension to students' musical learning.

The district holds its own elementary and secondary school music festivals for orchestra, chorus, and jazz and concert bands. The marching band consists of 175 students, all of whom attend band camp beginning in August. They perform throughout the year for football games and at competitions.

The general music program includes Piano Keyboard Lab and Movie Soundtrack Production. In a middle school keyboard class, for example, students compose music to accompany a music video, then perform and evaluate it. Special education students take particular advantage of the electronic keyboard classes and labs. They learn to work on the keyboards and write and record their thoughts through music. They also perform for parents and teachers. With this technology, these students excel in their study of music and performance, becoming part of the music community.

Music teachers attend monthly subject-specific staff development sessions to develop their music technology skills. Here teachers compare lesson plans and objectives, discuss challenges, and revise and update curriculum standards, striving to exceed state and national standards.

Parents are heavily involved in the music programs in the East Ramapo Central School District. Many help with the schools' musical productions and actively promote the district's music program.

Latest Developments

Since its recognition as a Model Music Program, the district's music program has flourished and has received recognition throughout the country. East Ramapo has created another music lab at the high school and is offering more music courses to students with special needs. The high school curriculum has broadened to include Music Theory and Movie Making.

The music technology program has thrived as well; since 2003, East Ramapo has expanded the use of music technology to all grades, with every teacher receiving training in technology. Teachers of intermediate students receive the music software program Smart Music.

DISCUSSION

These Model Music Programs—South Eastern School District, Haley Elementary School, and East Ramapo Central School District—show how schools can capitalize on the intrinsically engaging nature of both music and technology. Not one of these programs can be described in terms of technology only. They have strong band programs, amazing choral programs, or in-depth projects on world music. And all of them align curriculum and assessment according to both the National Standards and the standards of their respective states.

Technology comprises just one part of each program, but these programs use technology to support their philosophies on music education. Educators in the Model Music Programs don't exploit new technologies for the sake of filling their classrooms with new toys; they thoughtfully consider how they will excite, engage, and assist students in every aspect of their musical education, in addition to making routine daily tasks more efficient.

While analyzing the benefits and potential drawbacks of using technology in the music classroom is beyond the scope of this discussion, music educators and researchers generally agree that despite some negative aspects, technology, when used as part of a well-planned curriculum—especially one that incorporates the standards—positively affects students' motivation, engagement with the material, and learning efficiency.

Peter McCoy (2003) points out that "digital technologies are not a panacea for the music classroom; they are only useful to the extent that they allow students and teachers to function in ways that are faster or easier than before or to do things they could not do before" (p. 112). Haley Elementary School's music program, for example, has given up the messy, time-consuming blackboard in favor of digital media, and even student assessments are done digitally.

The potential to reach students otherwise uninterested in music is one of the most exciting aspects of deliberately integrating technology and music education. For example, high school students in East Ramapo Central School District must take the Keyboard/Computers course if they do not participate in a performance ensemble. Thus, every high school student is expected to create music in one form or another.

Technology exposes music to those who might not have an interest in music per se but like the "hands-on" element available in a technology class, especially in the upper grade levels. This tactile approach also resonates with many special learners, as the programs in South Eastern and East Ramapo indicated with their successes.

All of these Model Music Programs use computer software for composition. Although using MIDI technology for composition or improvisation is hardly the revolutionary activity that it was in the 1970s, these programs engage students in various, wide-ranging compositional activities that are relevant to their interests and sensitive to their individual creative strengths.

South Eastern School District's Kennard-Dale High School takes the basic composition activities offered in the introductory Music Technology course and introduces advanced projects like audio and video recording and editing. Students take ownership of their individual projects, become actively engaged in the process of creating music, and develop computer skills applicable to areas outside of music as well. Elementary students in Haley's music program compose pieces based on the letters that spell their names. Listening to their name composition excites young students because it personally relates to them.

Technology is expensive, though, and finding room in a tight budget for new technologies is tough. Wendy Bloom, music teacher at Haley Elementary School, sought technology grants. She took advantage of professional development opportunities specifically in technology that armed her with the right knowledge to make a case to Indiana's Department of Education that the money would be well spent. South Eastern School District compensated for the cost of upgrading the high school music labs by passing along the older computers to the middle schools and thus expanding the program while keeping labs up to date. East Ramapo, with a significantly larger music budget and per-pupil expenditure, ensures that students who don't participate in a performing group still engage in musical study by making technology part of the general music curriculum, and all students directly benefit from the music budget.

Another commonality among these schools is the effort of faculty to get and remain up to date with the latest developments in technology. For example, at East Ramapo, teachers attend monthly subject-specific staff development meetings that, among other things, develop their skills in technology. At Haley, Wendy Bloom works to keep up with what new technologies can offer. She describes her approach candidly, stating, "I like to think that I'm an old dog still learning some new tricks."

The three Model Music Programs described in this chapter represent an urban school (Haley Elementary School), a suburban district (East Ramapo

Central School District), and a rural community (South Eastern School District). Per-pupil expenditures range from $5,479 (South Eastern) to $7,470 (Haley) to $19,046 (East Ramapo). All three programs have very different circumstances and include technology differently, but each maximizes what it has to benefit as many students as possible.

Learning from Each Other

Interdisciplinary Learning and Cultural Music

Knowledge and culture are naturally interdisciplinary, and the study of music is particularly positioned to reach across various disciplines. The initial plan for this book was to separate programs into two chapters on interdisciplinary and multicultural music education, but it quickly became apparent that these two topics are impossibly intertwined when it comes to music.

Rather than containing the study of music to just the practice room or rehearsal hall, the programs in this chapter endeavor to make music relevant in all aspects of education. Page Middle School, Conners Emerson School, East Meadow Salisbury Center, and Nora Davis Magnet School connect music to diverse subjects and cultures, whether they originate halfway across the world in Ireland or from local Native American traditions and whether they have to do with literature or math. Though different in their approaches, these four programs cultivate interdisciplinary experiences for students, making them increasingly aware of how music is embedded in all aspects of culture in all parts of the world.

PAGE MIDDLE SCHOOL

Basic School Description

Page Middle School is located in rural Page, Arizona, close to the Utah state line. The city population is about 6,500, 50 percent of which is Native American, with 75 percent of the students at Page being Navajo. School buses go as far as forty-five to sixty miles south and east to bring students who live on the Navajo reservation to school. Page Middle School's enrollment is 685, and 70 percent of the students qualify for free or reduced lunch. The school has two full-time music teachers, and music teacher Janice Greisch submitted the program. The per-pupil expenditure is $6,000.

Budget and Other Funding

Page receives $3,700 for music, supplies, and teaching aides. The school budgets $5,000 for instruments and equipment and $3,000 for student activity travel and festival fees. Page has received additional funding in the form of grants and scholarships, such as a $2,800 At-Risk Student Grant from the National Dropout Prevention Program for the Native Cultures Music Club. The At-Risk Student Grant has been renewed for three years. The music program also receives $1,600 for summer music camp from Johnson O'Malley funds— a U.S. government program administered by local Indian Education Committees established "to provide supplementary financial assistance to meet the unique and specialized education needs of Indian children" (U.S. Office of Indian Education Programs, p. 8). In addition, funds for summer music camp scholarships include an additional $2,300 At-Risk Student Grant, $300 scholarships from the International Brotherhood of Electrical Workers, and $1,000 State of Arizona tax credit donations.

Scheduling

The music program offers six classes, including beginning, intermediate, and advanced levels of band. Sixth, seventh, or eighth graders may participate in any of the bands depending on their skill level. Page has a combined sixth-to-eighth-grade choir and five classes of general music for sixth-grade students.

Page offers eight classes of guitar for seventh and eighth graders at the beginning and intermediate levels. The school has three orchestra classes at the beginning, intermediate, and advanced levels. Students, regardless of grade level, may participate in an orchestra based on their skill level. All classes meet every other day for seventy minutes during the school day. With the exception of guitar, which lasts for one semester, all music classes are full-year courses.

Music Facilities and Equipment

Page Middle School has two music rooms specifically designed for music. The school also has one activity room designated exclusively for music classes, six practice rooms, and two music teacher offices. Three blocks away, on the high school campus, Page Middle School has access to an eight-hundred-seat auditorium that has a suspended wood floor stage that can accommodate a one-hundred-piece orchestra.

The music rooms have Wenger music stands and chairs. The program has approximately 80 wind instruments, 75 orchestral strings, 56 folk/classical guitars, 120 Native American flutes, and 1 electric guitar. Students can take advantage of twelve MIDI keyboards, a classroom set of Remo world-percussion instruments, five Orff xylophones, and mallet and battery percussion for marching. Each of the three classrooms also contains lockers to hold student instruments. Two have general sound systems, and the largest has a high-quality, recording-capable sound system.

Philosophy of Music Education

Page Middle School's music program is built on the philosophy that everyone deserves music education and that it constitutes an important part of each student's educational and life experience. The program organizes the curriculum according to Arizona State Standards for Music Education and the National Standards for the Arts. Students in each class and level have benchmark assessment levels that they are expected to achieve.

Unique Aspects of the Program

When Page Middle School changed to an A/B day (four plus four) block schedule ten years ago, music was deliberately kept as an indispensable part of the school's educational program. Two years ago, the school switched to five seventy-five-minute periods on each A and B day to meet new reading requirements.

Every sixth grader must take a music class, while music is an elective for the older students. Among many traditional musical opportunities, students can learn to play Native American flutes.

Outside of the school day, students may participate in a jazz band, a guitar club, the Native Cultures Music Club, and a Winter Guard International

Junior Percussion Team. School grants allow fifteen to twenty students annually to attend the Northern Arizona University Summer Music Camp.

Most remarkable, however, is the development of curricula to reflect the student population. Because 75 percent of the students are Navajo, the sixth-grade general music course examines world native cultures—their music, singing styles, and instruments. Students use Native American flutes, accompanied by world drums, guitar, and piano keyboard instruction.

Students study the native musical cultures of China, Polynesia, North and South America, and Africa in depth. They approach this music by emulating the style as closely as possible through singing and playing and by recognizing and analyzing the use of musical elements. The curriculum includes the study and application of the science of instrument sound production and making instruments. Students also improvise and compose melodies on Native American flutes and guitars in the style and tonal patterns of the music studied.

Latest Developments

Janice Greisch, the Page music teacher who submitted the school to the Model Music Program, retired in 2006, but she has remained involved with the school. She optimistically described Page's latest development as the commitment to continuing the music program. Because Page is in such a remote area, it is very difficult to attract teachers, especially in the arts. Greisch was not the only teacher to leave, so the principal, Eric Bonniksen, had a table at the 2006 MENC National Conference in an effort to contact people around the country to ensure that Page Middle School had music teachers.

According to Greisch, the central administration and school boards have given support both monetarily and visibly; many try to come to all of the concerts. The middle and high school orchestras recently performed their fall concert, and it was the best-attended and best-performed concert ever in Page. As Greisch commented, "this is quite exciting, since the orchestra program almost folded six years ago!"

CONNERS EMERSON SCHOOL

Basic School Description

Located on Mount Desert Island in Bar Harbor, Maine, Conners Emerson School is rural, public, and a combined elementary and middle school for students in kindergarten through eighth grade. Rebecca Edmondson submitted Conners Emerson to the Model Music Program competition. The school has two music teachers, 430 students, and a per-pupil expenditure of $7,507.

Budget and Other Funding

Both music teachers receive an annual budget of $900–$1,100. Of this budget, $300 goes toward instructional supplies and computer ink, $325 for printed music for all performing groups and music classes, and $200 for dues and conferences. This budget also pays for computer software and replacement of furniture.

The school receives other income from concert donations, private donations, PTSA support as requested, grants, and the Lip Sync Show, a fundraiser for stringed instruments and enrichment. The PTSA raises funds by having students sell wrapping paper, and the money goes to staff members for enrichment of their programs rather than a budget item. Concert donations typically bring in about $100. The Mount Desert Island School Union 98 offers instruction grants, such as a $770 grant to develop a unit called "Voices of the Underground Railroad." For the past several years, the Conners Emerson music program has received an anonymous $1,000 donation, which is used by the music teachers at their discretion.

At the Lip Sync Show, individual students or small ensembles choose music to which they add routines, costumes, and lip sync. Admission is $1 for students and $3 for parents. Proceeds, along with a parent-organized bake sale, generate $700–$800. The money raised sometimes is designated for a specific item (such as second-grade class violins or a string bass) and sometimes goes toward the maintenance of school instruments or toward hosting guest musicians for enrichment.

Scheduling

At Conners Emerson, kindergarten students have general music for thirty-five minutes once weekly. Grades 1–4 have general music for forty minutes each week. Grades 5–8 have eighty minutes of general music twice each week for one trimester. In addition to general music, fourth-grade beginning band and third- and fourth-grade string orchestra rehearse for thirty minutes once each week (during recess), and the fifth- through eighth-grade full orchestra rehearses for thirty-five minutes, twice each week (during study hall). Fifth- to

sixth-grade band and seventh- to eighth-grade band rehearse forty-five minutes twice per week. The chorus (grades 5–8) rehearses thirty-five minutes
twice per week. The Swallowtail Fiddlers practice once each week for twenty
minutes before school, and the jazz band meets for forty-five minutes before
school three times per week.

Conners Emerson has a full performance schedule for each grade level.
Second-grade class violin, fourth-grade band, and third- and fourth-grade string
orchestra have performances in winter and spring. All K–4 music classes sing and
dance in the spring concerts. The fifth- through eighth-grade full orchestra has
two concerts in addition to a performance at the Maine Music Educators Association Large Group Festival. The Conners Emerson Orchestra has the prestige
of being the only orchestra in the state to perform at this event. The Swallowtail
Fiddlers perform at concerts and community events and provide community
service through fundraisers and playing at homes for the aged.

Students in first- through fourth-grade choruses, fifth- and sixth-grade
band, seventh- and eighth-grade band, and the fifth- through eighth-grade
chorus also perform at two annual concerts. A fifth- and sixth-grade jazz band
performs each spring, and the seventh- and eighth-grade jazz band performs
at two concerts, a district festival, and a state competition.

Music Facilities and Equipment

Conners Emerson School has one large music room (38′ × 31′) for all music classes, orchestras, bands, and choruses that opens as a stage into the gym.
The program also has one small music room (7′ × 23′) for instrumental lessons. Both rooms have a piano.

The school has twenty violins in varying sizes, six cellos, three basses, approximately forty-five assorted band instruments, a keyboard, and three upright pianos. Many students rent or own their instruments, but the available
inventory allows students with financial difficulties to borrow a school instrument. A music store representative services instruments once a week and does
minor repairs at the school. Other equipment includes music stands, chairs, a
computer, and instrumental and choral risers.

Philosophy of Music Education

The Conners Emerson music program describes music education in
terms of purpose, aiming for the development of lifelong musical under-

standing, skill, and sensitivity in students' lives. Based on the belief that each person has some musical ability, Conners Emerson's program has definitive goals: all music students will know that music has duration, pitch, form, timbre, and expressive qualities; feel the emotional content that music expresses; possess some understanding of their own musical heritage as well as that of other cultures; and grow continually in their ability to listen and respond to, appreciate, evaluate, and create music with understanding, skill, and sensitivity.

Bar Harbor, a community made up of many nationalities, provides excellent opportunities for students to create music that resonates with everyone in ensembles *and* audiences. Songs and dances of many cultures comprise central elements of the ensembles' repertoire.

Unique Aspects of the Program

Young, dedicated musicians begin their string instruction in grade 2 class violin. Conners Emerson provides every second grader with a violin for music class and performances as a hands-on approach to reading music. Three classes share these instruments. Class violin is a core academic subject and is also performance based.

The Conners Emerson string program now reaps the benefits of the grade 2 class violin. Orchestra numbers grew at the middle school level, and the Conners Emerson Middle School Orchestra is one of very few full orchestras in the state of Maine.

As a continuation of reading and playing music, a portion of third-grade music class is devoted to learning to play the tin whistle. The tin whistles are in the key of D to allow students to easily combine the whistles and violins (or fiddles) in performances with mixed grades. In fourth grade, students may choose a band instrument in addition to playing a string instrument.

The Swallowtail Fiddlers is a multi-age fiddling club formed in the 2002–2003 school year with only four members. This club has quadrupled in number with members who play violins, viola, cello, and tin whistle while the music teacher provides guitar accompaniment. Students in the club perform traditional folk music at various community places and events. Their repertoire consists of toe-tapping jigs, reels, hornpipes, and ditties of America, Ireland, and Scotland. Open to any motivated student in third through eighth

The Swallowtail Fiddlers from the Conners Emerson School play at their weekly practice session under the direction of Rebecca Edmondson.

grade seeking an alternative avenue of cultural expression, the Swallowtail Fiddlers meet once a week before school.

There is a strong tradition of folk and Irish music on Mount Desert Island and the Downeast Maine area. Many small bands in the area have formed to supply music for country, square, and contra dances and pub music. Fiddlers easily fit in all of these styles. In Bar Harbor, Maine, it is not uncommon to see young children making music in a band with their grandparents. In forming the Swallowtail Fiddlers, the hope was to create a learning environment through which students could learn traditional music styles and apply them to real-life experience. Fiddling has also sparked new enthusiasm for the violin, and folk music has enhanced the string program at Conners Emerson School.

According to music teacher Rebecca Edmondson, "it is important that we try to include everyone in our program and meet the needs of young musicians." Because Mount Desert Island has a biology laboratory that brings researchers from all parts of the world, every effort is made to expose students to the diverse cultures in the Conners Emerson School population. Many of the songs and dances students learn reflect the heritage of the students. The program combines song and dance to allow for the integration of disciplines. As Edmondson points out, "the history of a people is found in its music, and music reflects the environment and cultural influence of its time." Though Edmondson is classically trained in oboe and piano, she draws on her own background by playing Scottish bagpipes and Irish tin whistle to breathe life into centuries-old folk music with her students.

Latest Developments

With the MENC grant they received for their designation as a Model Music Program, Conners Emerson School bought a viola and a recording system, which has served them well as an accurate documentation of student performance and a motivational tool. First through fourth graders were recorded singing "The Star-Spangled Banner" (first graders sang the first verse, second graders the second verse, and so on). As a service learning project, CDs were distributed to sports coaches to play before competitions and to MENC as Conners Emerson's contribution to the National Anthem Project. The Swallowtail Fiddlers recorded a CD, which they sold to raise $900 for a local family in need facing large medical bills.

Each year, Edmondson provides enrichment for her string students, such as hosting the maestro from the Bangor Symphony Orchestra to conduct workshops with the middle school full orchestra, elementary strings, and second-grade class violin. The school also received funding from the PTSA to commission a composer from the University of Maine at Orono to compose a piece for the Emerson Middle School full orchestra. "There is so much at Conners Emerson School in which we can take pride," says Edmondson. "We really make a schoolwide effort to offer as much music education as time permits. Everyone—the parents, volunteers, teachers, administrators, and students—can be very proud of what we accomplish in our schools."

EAST MEADOW SCHOOL DISTRICT

Basic School Description

East Meadow School District serves the students of East Meadow and Westbury, New York, two suburbs of Manhattan. The district has five elementary schools: Barnum Woods, Bowling Green, George McVey, Meadowbrook, and

Parkway; two middle schools: Woodland and W. Tresper Clarke; and two high schools: East Meadow and W. Tresper Clarke. The district has thirty-nine full-time music teachers and supervisors. The total per-pupil expenditure is $15,018.

Budget and Other Funding

For the nine schools in the district, East Meadow budgets $40,500 for supplies, $31,812 for festivals and contests, $63,229 for repair, $101,025 for equipment (plus $75,000 for a new computer lab and recording equipment), $2,296 for an artist-in-residence, and $87,882 for the Arts in Education Program.

Outside of the budget, the district's music programs also received a $10,000 Empire State Partnerships Grant with the American Symphony Orchestra.

Scheduling

In East Meadow's elementary schools, students in grades 1–3 participate in general music thirty minutes twice per week. Fourth and fifth graders have general music forty-five minutes once per week. Fourth-grade beginning band, orchestra, and chorus meet forty to fifty minutes once per week. (Some schools combine fourth- and fifth-grade chorus.) Fifth-grade band, orchestra, and chorus meet forty to fifty minutes twice per week. Each fourth- and fifth-grade student can take band, orchestra, chorus, band and chorus, or orchestra and chorus in addition to their general music classes.

In the middle schools, band, orchestra, and chorus students have rehearsals every other day. Students may take only one music class during the regular school day, including general music. They also participate in a rotating weekly small group lesson for band and orchestra and every twelve days for vocal students. General music meets every other day for one period. Middle school students can participate in after-school ensembles, such as instrumental and vocal jazz or the string ensemble.

High school students may take as many music classes as they can fit into their schedule. Band, orchestra, and chorus rehearsals meet for one period every day. Like the middle school students, high school instrumental and vocal students participate in rotating weekly small group lessons. Other courses include Music Theory I and II and Advanced Theory, Music Production and

Recording, Jazz Improvisation, and Chamber Music. Each of these meets for one period every day.

Music Facilities and Equipment

All East Meadow School District band programs have Wenger chairs and stands, a full complement of percussion equipment (including timpani and mallet percussion), marching and concert band instruments, tuners, metronomes, a computer, a music library, a stereo, and a piano. The orchestras have Wenger chairs and stands, a full complement of string instruments, tuners, metronomes, a computer, a music library, a piano, and a stereo. Choral facilities have choral risers, a piano, a computer, a music library, and a stereo.

Elementary and middle schools recently received new xylophones. All middle and high schools received marimbas. The district also purchased seventeen additional half-sized violas for its blossoming elementary string program. Both high schools and one middle school have Mac computer labs and recording studios. All elementary and middle schools have MIE keyboard labs.

Philosophy of Music Education

East Meadow School District's music program is based on the hope that students' involvement with music in school will give them a solid foundation for a lifetime of appreciation of music and enriching musical opportunities. Through the processes of practice, rehearsal, and performance, the district administration and music teachers believe students will develop self-discipline, enhanced cooperation skills, and an increased ability to listen to and follow directions. They can carry these skills into many other facets of their lives.

Unique Aspects of the Program

East Meadow School District offers a five-week summer music program for students who completed third grade through seniors in high school. The beginner instrumental program for grades 4–6 offers students daily lessons and supervised practice sessions on all stringed instruments (modified Suzuki program), flute, clarinet, trumpet, French horn, trombone, baritone horn, and tuba. After three weeks of daily lessons, the supervised practice sessions evolve into a beginning band and orchestra.

East Meadow School District conducted a string residency program with the New York Virtuosi Chamber Orchestra.

The district has had a string residency program with the New York Virtuosi Chamber Orchestra and now has a "side-by-side" program with members of the American Symphony Orchestra where students rehearse and perform "side by side" with professional musicians. Students participate in the Global Encounters and LinkUP! Programs through Carnegie Hall's Education Program, and many have taken part in master classes with members of the New York Philharmonic, Bobby McFerrin, and other noted artists. Students at all grade levels have had the opportunity to play several pieces commissioned for them. East Meadow School District has a composer-in-residence, Carl Strommen.

Staff development is provided for teachers, and they deliberately integrate music curriculum with other disciplines. For example, through the district's Empire State Partnerships Grant with the American Symphony Orchestra, students attend their thematic concerts and preconcert lectures. In an inter-disciplinary manner that includes English, social studies, and art, students learn the historical background of a concert before attending. In English

East Meadow School District has a partnership grant with the American Symphony Orchestra, and professional musicians rehearse and perform side by side with the students.

classes, students explore different writing projects, including poetry. Student artwork based on a concert's theme was displayed at Lincoln Center during an American Symphony Orchestra concert at Avery Fisher Hall. This program is offered to all students, not just music students.

Another example of interdisciplinary learning occurred when composer Mark Camphouse visited the district to work with members of the high school bands, faculty, and alumni. Because students performed his piece, "A Movement for Rosa," the music chairperson arranged for social studies classes to come to the rehearsal, and he spoke about Rosa Parks and the civil rights movement.

Latest Developments

Both of East Meadow School District's high schools were recently named Grammy Signature School finalists once again. The East Meadow High School Marching Band won the New York City Columbus Day parade again, for a total of eight first-place wins. The W. Tresper Clarke High School Tri-M chapter was named as National Tri-M Chapter of the Year, and they were part of a panel at Tri-M sessions at the New York State School Music Association conference in Rochester, New York, and the Eastern Division Conference in Hartford, Connecticut. Finally, East Meadow's partnership grant with the American Symphony Orchestra was increased to $25,000.

NORA DAVIS MAGNET SCHOOL

Basic School Description

Nora Davis Magnet School is part of the Laurel School District in Laurel, Mississippi. It's a rural public elementary school with 301 students and 1 full-time music teacher. Jodie Austin submitted the school to the Model Music Program competition. The school's per-pupil expenditure is $8,000.

Budget and Other Funding

The school system does not have a specific budget for the Music Department at Nora Davis, but the school always receives what it needs through the general fund. Nora Davis has received funding from the Whole Schools Initiative Model Schools, activity funds, and fund-raising efforts. Once certain programs got off the ground and the community saw their value, local business and individuals were willing to fund activities like the school's opera and the Cultural Arts Festival. Additionally, selling T-shirts and producing the opera, musical, and holiday show raise funds.

Scheduling

Grades K–2 have thirty minutes of general music weekly. Third graders have forty-five minutes of general music each week, and fourth through sixth graders have forty minutes of general music. Twice per week, fifty students in grades 4–6 participate in show choir for forty-five minutes. These students also devote eighty minutes per week to the opera in the fall and the musical in the spring. Twenty sixth graders in beginning band rehearse during the school day for forty minutes two to three times each week.

Nora Davis also has a Music Infusion Day for which the music specialist and classroom teachers collaborate. One day each week, the music specialist goes to all the sections of one particular grade level. She meets with each grade level throughout the year for a period of about five weeks. (Music Infusion Day is discussed later in greater detail.)

Music Facilities and Equipment

Nora Davis has a large general music room. They recently acquired Wenger folding risers that are used for sitting, standing, and as a stage for drama. The school has a soundboard, six body microphones, and a karaoke machine. Available instruments include rhythm and Orff instruments and two pianos. Equipment gets replaced as needed, assuming funds are available.

Philosophy of Music Education

According to Nora Davis Magnet School's mission statement, the school aims to promote confident, self-directed, lifelong learners while creating an atmosphere where learning is the primary focus. The school believes that music is essential for students to learn to express themselves. They become confident in performance and dedicate themselves to working, learning, and performing with a group.

Nora Davis aligns curriculum, goals, and expectations with the National Standards for Music Education. Students discover the relationships among music, other arts, and disciplines outside of the arts through collaborative efforts. Nora Davis students also come to understand music in relation to history and culture through the school's annual Cultural Arts Festival.

Unique Aspects of the Program

Nora Davis Magnet School gives students many opportunities to perform. A beginning band serves twenty sixth-grade students, and a beginning strings program serves about twenty students in first through sixth grades. Rehearsals are held during the school day to allow more students to participate, and these groups perform for local festivals, clubs, service organizations, and the local hospital. The band, strings, and show choir groups join with visual art and dance to perform an Arts Explosion exhibit each year for the school and community.

Nora Davis has been a part of the Mississippi Whole Schools Initiative, Mississippi's first comprehensive statewide arts education program, for seven years and a Model School for Whole Schools for the past two years. The Whole Schools Initiative has five goals: (1) to improve student achievement through the infusion of arts into the basic curriculum, (2) to enrich the lives of students through knowledge and skills in all arts disciplines, (3) to assist professional and personal growth of teachers through arts experiences, (4) to use the arts to increase parental and community involvement with schools, and (5) to assist schools in building a sustainable system for supporting arts infusion.

Music Infusion Day particularly sets Nora Davis apart from other schools. In a collaborative planning effort, the arts specialist and classroom teachers at each grade level determine the content students should master. The classroom teachers and music specialist choose a skill that is either being introduced or one proving difficult for students to grasp. Teachers choose a skill on any subject and the music specialist figures out how to present it in a musical way. Students are then presented with both the general curriculum concept and an arts concept. The specialist also ensures that the lesson reinforces a musical skill or meets a National Standard.

Nora Davis also holds an annual Cultural Arts Festival. The school chooses one culture or country as its focus for an entire day and endeavors to celebrate a culture that is of relevance at the time. For example, in the wake of Hurricane Katrina, the festival focused on the culture of New Orleans. The next year's festival celebrated Polynesian culture.

Prior to the festival, students and teachers work on incorporating the culture into the curriculum. In music, students study the culture's musical heritage, listen to the music, and discuss instruments commonly used. In dance classes, students do the same thing with that art form. In the regular classroom, teachers find ways to incorporate the culture's history, geography, and so on. Nora Davis secures guest artists—musicians, dancers, and visual artists—to visit on the day of the festival.

By the time the day arrives, students already have a lot of knowledge about most of the things they will see, but the Cultural Arts Festival brings that knowledge to life. About eight to ten hands-on stations include such activities as instrument making, food tasting, storytelling, dancing, and jewelry making. The close of the day culminates in a huge parade with students listening and marching to music of the culture, doing dances they have learned, and displaying the things they have made during the day.

Latest Developments

Nora Davis is working hard to make classroom teacher training a top priority and wants classroom teachers to feel comfortable using music, dance, and visual art in their classrooms every day. Teachers spend a lot of time in staff development discussing appropriate terminology and vocabulary to empower them when using the arts as a teaching tool.

For another new project, Nora Davis students created a Christmas CD with the equipment the school had available. Students rehearsed for weeks, auditions were held for solos, and the department gathered support from the PTA and community. The endeavor was an overwhelming success. Though not a perfect CD (music specialist Jodie Austin notes that you'll hear a cough or sneeze now and again), teachers felt it was a tremendous learning experience. Older students even had the opportunity to learn about the recording process and equipment used.

DISCUSSION

The sometimes politically charged topic of "multicultural education" has many definitions, and its proponents and opponents have varying agendas. Nonetheless, partly because districts have endeavored to mandate multicultural education across all disciplines, teachers in different departments collaborate more than ever, showing how all disciplines connect to each other.

"Whatever the perspective, demographic or the purely musical, the music taught and learned in schools spans a much wider spectrum than it did even [two decades] ago," comments Patricia Shehan Campbell (1996, p. 1). Page Middle School, Conners Emerson School, East Meadow School District, and Nora Davis Magnet School teach music for the sake of music as well as a mode for teaching in other disciplines. After all, the very act of learning the music of another country requires knowing a certain amount about its people, history, culture, and environment, among other things—thus cultural and world music is inherently interdisciplinary to a degree.

Some have criticized the term *multicultural* or the certain political or educational elements of multicultural education, but the purpose of the term within the current context of this book is to reveal the incredibly huge range of musical cultures that this idea encompasses. Within these four programs, students thoroughly study cultures outside the United States, such as those in Polynesia, Ireland, and Scotland, and those a bit more local, such as Arizona and New Orleans. And, as one teacher pointed out, even the band or orchestra music so familiar to many of us is an entirely foreign cultural expression to many students.

East Meadow's music program is deliberately interdisciplinary. Music, social studies, and English classes merge on a particular curriculum unit. The option of all students—not just music students—to attend the educational programs of the American Symphony orchestra exposes them to a cultural event tied to American history.

The schools or districts in this chapter collaborate and explore various musics based largely on their demographics. Seventy-five percent of Page Middle School students are Navajo, for instance, and learning to play Native American flutes is part of the general music curriculum. At Page, 85 percent of band students are white, while 95 percent of guitar and orchestra students are Native American. According to retired music chair Janice Greisch, many students live remotely (some travel up to sixty miles to attend school) with no neighbors for up to ten miles; playing the guitar is something they can excel at on their own.

Based on her thirty-five years of experience, observation, and comments from students, Greisch notes her Navajo students tend to choose instruments based on their own preferences of timbre and method of performance because orchestra is unfamiliar to this isolated area and students have no preconceived ideas of what is popular. For these students, orchestra constitutes a music study of a different culture. Additionally, students in sixth-grade general music focus intensively on world native cultures—their music, singing styles, and instruments. The school's art club painted a world map mural on the music room wall with representative instruments located on the countries. Even for students already familiar with particular native cultures or their instruments, students benefit from the cross-disciplinary quality of the curriculum.

Conners Emerson is similar to Page in that its music program takes advantage of local culture. Like Page integrating Navajo flutes into its general music curriculum, the string program builds a repertoire of folk music, among other styles, that students may use in the community. Music teacher Rebecca Edmondson's comment bears repeating: in Bar Harbor, Maine, children commonly perform with grandparents or other family members.

Nora Davis Magnet School infuses the arts into all disciplines—even math. There, kindergarteners benefit from the classroom teacher and music specialist working cooperatively to teach both musical concepts and math concepts simultaneously. Fourth- through sixth-grade students participate in the Metropolitan Opera Guild's "Creating Original Opera" Program in the fall and produce a Broadway Junior Show in the spring. In both cases, Dance, Visual Art, and Drama Departments work in conjunction with the Music Department.

All four of these programs indicate a strong theme of collaboration among teachers. For example, the Nora Davis music specialist not only meets with the classroom teacher to discuss curriculum and lesson plans, but she also equips the classroom teacher to teach music concepts accurately when "infusing" them into other curricula.

3

Music for All

For many years, music teachers realized that music had the ability to resonate with typical students and students with disabilities in ways that other academic subjects might not.

Providing students with disabilities with a musical education became law with Congress's decision to pass the Individuals with Disabilities Education Act (IDEA—Public Law 94–142, 1975). The law mandated that "each school system shall take steps to ensure that its handicapped children have available to them the same variety of educational programs and services available to nonhandicapped children served by the school, including art, music, industrial arts, [and] consumer and vocational education" (P.L. 94–142, as cited in Brown 2000, p. 26).

More recently, the Americans with Disabilities Act (ADA) was passed in 1990 to ensure broad civil rights protections, and an updated version of IDEA was passed in 2004 to reauthorize the original law and increase accountability. These federal laws, MENC's mission to advance music education by encouraging the study and making of music by all, and the philosophies held by all twelve of the Model Music Programs are in agreement when it comes to musically serving America's students with special needs.

This chapter examines how two extremely different programs strive to make music a part of every child's life. Though very, very different from each

other, the Spurwink School and the William Floyd School District both constitute valuable examples of how music can enrich the lives of all students.

THE SPURWINK SCHOOL: ROOSEVELT PROGRAM

Basic School Description

The Spurwink School is a nonprofit, private special-needs school located in
South Portland, Maine. The Roosevelt Program is just one of Spurwink's therapeutic day treatment programs. The student body of this particular Spurwink program is made up of fifty-five elementary and middle school students
who did not find success in public schools due to various behavioral, developmental, and severe cognitive challenges. All of Spurwink's students are referred from public schools through the special education process, and all
students have individualized education programs (IEPs). The school has one
part-time music teacher, Jeff Shaw, who teaches at Spurwink's Roosevelt Program three days per week and submitted the program. The school has a student-to-teacher ratio of 2 to 1.

Budget and Other Funding

Spurwink budgets $1,500 for music annually. This is used to purchase in-
struments, such as electric guitars and amplifiers, and various instrument ac-
cessories, such as guitar strings, guitar picks, patch cords, drumsticks, and so
on. As Spurwink experiments with digital recording technology, some of the
budgeted amount goes toward hardware and software. Also, due to space and
sound level issues, some of the budget is allocated for renting off-site studio
space where students go for drum lessons once per week.

The music program and teacher are funded through the school budget,
which is based on an annual rate-setting process. The school acquires no other
funding. The Spurwink School is funded by Maine's Department of Education and various branches of the Department of Health and Human Services,
and mental health funding comes from Medicaid (MaineCare).

Scheduling

Scheduling at Spurwink is more fluid than for typical music programs.
Classes and lessons adapt to the level of cognitive, developmental, and behavioral functioning of each student. Every student has the opportunity to take

one-on-one or small-group instrument lessons in a way that he or she can. The individual lessons last for fifteen to twenty minutes, and the small-group lessons are thirty to sixty minutes. Although Spurwink has a set schedule, the music teacher tries to keep things flexible due to the nature of the school. For example, if a classroom is experiencing behavior problems or going on a special field trip, then the teacher reschedules his music class. Likewise, if a student is scheduled to have a one-on-one lesson but is having a difficult day or did not do his or her homework, the lesson is rescheduled.

Music Facilities and Equipment

The basement of the school has a room that serves as the music and art room. It is approximately 12′ × 19′ with brick walls, exposed pipes, painted cement floors, and two windows. Individual lessons are often given in the music room, occupational therapy room, or an off-site studio.

One of the classroom teachers is on the board of directors at a local playhouse that allows Spurwink to use its facility to host its talent shows. The theater seats nearly three hundred and is complete with a stage, lighting system, and dressing rooms—and the kids love it.

The Spurwink School.

Spurwink's music program began in 2004, and at that time, the school received $20,000 from the state to procure the instruments and materials that the newly hired music teacher deemed necessary. Spurwink's percussion instruments include congas, djembes, bongos, frame drums, tambourines, egg shakers, maracas, sleigh bells, triangles, guiros, claves, vibraslaps, xylophones, glockenspiels, and a five-piece drum set. The school has three acoustic steel string guitars, three acoustic classical guitars, three baritone ukuleles, and thirty recorders. Electronic equipment includes an electric keyboard with MIDI capability, a laptop computer, stereo, and record player. Instruments such as a piano, keyboard, amplifier, and hand drum were donated to the school.

Philosophy of Music Education

Spurwink aims to approximate the standard curriculum of the public schools, and this includes music. In developing its music program, Spurwink sought to integrate the principles of the National Standards for Music Education and the Maine State Learning Results while remaining mindful of the students' unique needs and limitations. The program measures student achievement largely by students' levels of enjoyment and their investment in the program. Teachers care less about making sure that students sing the correct note than they do about the fact that they do sing. The Spurwink program focuses on motivating students to discover the value of learning new skills with an art previously foreign to them.

Unique Aspects of the Program

Spurwink music teacher Jeff Shaw says that the students constitute the most unique aspect of the Spurwink School. As he describes the school, "from autism to schizophrenia, from the learning disabled to students struggling with emotional difficulties, all of them find a desk at our institution." Spurwink provides its students with extra care and attention unavailable in more traditional educational settings. These philosophies guided the development of the new music program.

In the past, teachers and staff members had to take it upon themselves to bring music to the students, resulting in an occasional sing-along or instrument demonstration. Spurwink finally secured funding for a music teacher. Most students had never taken a music class, and the new teacher created a program from scratch. While traditional music programs focus on areas such as performance and theory, Spurwink grounds its program in creativity and fostering positive musical experiences for students.

The music program produces talent shows, constituting the first opportunity for Spurwink students' families, friends, and counselors to attend a performance. Despite limitations imposed by confidentiality restrictions (Spurwink cannot open performances up to the public, announce students' names on stage, or print their names in the programs), the events have gone wonderfully.

Latest Developments

After MENC recognized Spurwink as a Model Music Program, the school bought a new MacBook Pro for the music department with the grant money. This allows the director to record music that Spurwink students create and burn CDs for them to take home and share with their friends, family, and staff.

WILLIAM FLOYD SCHOOL DISTRICT

Basic District Description

William Floyd School District in Mastic Beach, New York, has a total school population of 10,511 students, with 43 full-time music teachers and supervisors. The district consist of five elementary schools, two middle schools, and a very large high school complex divided into a 9/10 building and an 11/12 building, both part of William Floyd High School. Per-pupil expenditure is $16,339.

Budget and Other Funding

The music budget for the elementary, middle, and high schools totals $93,425.99. This includes $30,000 allocated for instrument repair and $19,288 for professional development and attendance at county, state, and national conferences.

Fund-raising occurs at the middle school and high school levels. These funds go toward participation in music competitions, extracurricular cultural events, and the purchase of items not within school budgetary codes.

Additionally, the PTO supports the music program through flower sales and raffles at the winter and spring concerts. Funds from these efforts were used to purchase a baby grand piano for the high school auditorium that was needed for the district's performing groups' concerts and a complete sound system with recording capabilities for the sound booth in the auditorium. Grants from the PTO and district have allowed for upgrades and the implementation of technology at the elementary and secondary levels.

The Board of Cooperative Education in the state of New York provides cultural arts funding that the music departments use for professional development, musical theater productions, guest conductors for the All-District Elementary Festival, and commissioned works.

Scheduling

Students in kindergarten through fifth grade have two forty-minute music classes each week. In addition to general music, fourth- and fifth-grade band students have two sixty-minute rehearsals per week. Chorus and orchestra begin in third grade, with two sixty-minute class periods weekly, in addition to general music. Band, orchestra, and chorus are scheduled separately to avoid limiting students' performance experiences. Beginners' band and the Recorder Club also begin in third grade, meeting for forty minutes once per week after school.

In the middle schools, class periods are 40 minutes, and the following classes meet for 2.5 periods weekly: general music, band, chorus, and orchestra. The chamber orchestra, jazz band, and select chorus meet for one hour one day after school.

At the high school, the following classes meet five times weekly for forty minutes: three bands, two choruses, two orchestras, three piano classes, and Theory I, II, III, and IV. Two jazz ensembles, one select jazz choir, one select choir, and two chamber orchestras meet once per week for two hours.

Music Facilities and Equipment

In both the band and orchestra programs, the district provides all necessary instruments for students to use at school, allowing students to have a practice instrument at home. Rehearsal areas have a complete set of Wenger lockers for instrument and music storage. Rooms have a complete audio system with recording capabilities. Section leaders have a master tuner and individual tuners. Rooms contain Wenger stands and chairs, and the middle and high school rehearsal rooms have pianos.

Every choral rehearsing area has Wenger storage, chairs, and choral risers. The rooms have a full audio system with recording capabilities. Middle and high schools have lesson areas as well.

General music classrooms in the elementary schools have a piano, full Orff instrumentation, rhythm instruments, and hand bells. Secondary classrooms have twenty-five MIDI-capable keyboards, thirty-five guitars, and complete world drumming percussion. Wenger lockers store instruments. Each room has access to individual computers with software for composing and performing using MIDI-capable synthesizers.

Philosophy of Music Education

The William Floyd School District Music Department has identified essential learning in all subject areas at all grade levels, clarifying what knowledge and skills students should develop. Instead of asking, "Where are students compared to their classmates?" teachers now ask, "Where are students in relation to the grade-level learning goals and expectations?"

William Floyd School District holds the philosophy that strong elementary school programs lead to continued interest at the middle and high school levels. Thus, students enroll in performance groups (band, orchestra, and chorus) in third grade, in addition to their general music classes. At William Floyd, performing groups practice a pedagogy of sequential development with multiple opportunities for musical expression and appreciation of mediums rich in cultural and historic literature.

The district has implemented a thorough system of assessment at all areas and levels of music instruction, establishing expectations of specific knowledge and standards of performance at each stage of development. Assessment requires students to apply the skills they have developed, demonstrate the knowledge they have gained, respond to feedback, and critique their own work.

Unique Aspects of the Program

All students can participate in summer music. Select honor groups exist at all levels, such as brass ensemble, wind ensemble, percussion ensemble in band, string ensemble, chamber groups in orchestra, and select choirs. William Floyd School District has a full jazz program consisting of jazz bands, ensembles, and choirs for grades 6–12. Every year, William Floyd holds an All-

District Elementary Festival featuring the band, chorus, and orchestra members of the district's elementary schools. In 2003, William Floyd High School commissioned and premiered a composition titled "Passing Strangers" by Pulitzer Prize–winning composer Norman Dello Joio.

The William Floyd Community Out-Reach Program brings live music to numerous venues throughout the community. The faculty of the district's Music Department "practice what they preach" by presenting an annual faculty concert to raise funds for music scholarships.

William Floyd School District is one of very few schools in New York State to have an Adaptive Music Program. This inclusive program provides services for students with special needs to explore and appreciate music. In this program, a two-teacher team (one art and one music), both with dual certification in (1) art or music and (2) special education, music therapy, or art therapy, works with students with severe disabilities in self-contained, non-mainstreamed classes consisting of fewer than twelve students each. The focus of the program is therapeutic and experiential.

In the Adaptive Arts Program, music and art experiences are chosen based upon the needs identified in a student's IEP. The special education teacher and the Adaptive Team design goals for these students. All students receive multiple performance experiences on band instruments and string instruments as well as through singing and movement. The Adaptive Team has an independent budget controlled by the fine arts director for supplies, equipment, and instruments. The Special Education Office supplies a budget for professional development of the Adaptive Team to explore effective pedagogy and other research on education for this special population.

Latest Developments

William Floyd School District's Music Department recently completed their districtwide improvement plan for the 2006–2007 and 2007–2008 school years. The department has also developed a committee to design an instructional observation model and a teacher evaluation model aligned with the department's learning expectations.

DISCUSSION

The most obvious difference between the Spurwink School and the William Floyd School District is the type of students who attend the schools. Spurwink caters to the special-needs student exclusively, while William Floyd is a typical public school district for all students. Though William Floyd has high expectations and a standards-based music curriculum, students with severe disabilities receive an individualized musical education in which they have the opportunity to explore and experience various forms of music. Likewise, Spurwink tailors music education to each of its students, helping them find success through different pedagogical approaches. This support and customization for special-needs students characterizes the fundamental similarity in how Spurwink and William Floyd approach teaching these students.

William Floyd's Adaptive Music Program is but one extraordinary element of a strong, comprehensive, standards-based program. Elementary students receive limitless musical opportunities, and all of the district's performing groups perform at a superior level. High-quality music education at every level is what makes William Floyd a Model Music Program. The Adaptive Music Program reflects the district's commitment to providing each student the opportunity to not only participate but also *excel* in music.

While Spurwink and William Floyd both customize curriculum for students with special needs, Spurwink does so on a smaller scale. With only fifty-five students, Spurwink can remain extremely flexible to students' individual needs while maintaining a predictable, supportive environment.

Jeff Shaw, Spurwink's music teacher, has the goal of providing a music experience that mirrors the experience his students would have in a regular school setting, but he tailors his classes to the group's level of functioning. For example, if it is "Guitar Day," lower-functioning classes learn how many strings a guitar has, its different parts, how it makes its sound, and each student gets a chance to strum the strings or play a few notes. A higher-functioning class learns more about the history of the instrument, how it is built, who some famous guitarists are, and how to play a chord or simple scale. The pace at which Shaw covers material, particularly in small-group or individual lessons, depends on the aptitude of students.

The integration of technology also helps students with special needs. As Spurwink students have started to experiment with recordings, it is worth reminding readers of the success students with special needs found through the music and technology programs at South Eastern School District and East Ramapo (chapter 1).

The music programs at the Spurwink School and the William Floyd School District exhibit how even students with special needs can experience high-quality music education when well-qualified, committed teachers meet each student where he or she is emotionally, cognitively, and physically.

4

Standards-Based Programs

Each model program recognized in this publication structures its program in relation to the National Standards. Through the articulation of their curriculum and program structure, the model programs reflect the implementation of the National Standards as well as state standards.

In 1994, the Goals 2000: Educate America Act formally recognized the arts (music, dance, theater, and visual arts) as a fundamental academic subject. Led by MENC, the Consortium of National Arts Education Associations developed the National Standards for Arts Education that delineate what students should "know and be able to do in the arts."

According to the Consortium of National Arts Education Association (1994), having a set of standards for the arts "combat[s] the uniformed idea that the arts are an 'academically soft' area of study" (p. 15). More importantly, they guide music instruction so that students receive the best education and perform at the highest levels. In so doing, the standards provide a foundation for assessment. Former MENC president Paul Lehman (2000) describes the National Standards as a "basic framework for all music teaching that is applicable in every setting regardless of how much or how little time the teacher has" (p. 4).

The Music Content Standards for grades K–12 are:

1. Singing, alone and with others, a varied repertoire of music.
2. Performing on instruments, alone and with others, a varied repertoire of music.

3. Improvising melodies, variations, and accompaniments.
4. Composing and arranging music within specified guidelines.
5. Reading and notating music.
6. Listening to, analyzing, and describing music.
7. Evaluating music and music performance.
8. Understanding relationships between music, the other arts, and disciplines outside the arts.
9. Understanding music in relation to history and culture.

Actual implementation of the National Standards for music education nationwide requires future research, but the music programs at Adlai E. Stevenson High School, Rutland County Schools, and Nanuet Union Free School District provide examples of how other programs can emulate the integration of standards into their existing curriculum.

ADLAI E. STEVENSON HIGH SCHOOL

Basic School Description

Adlai E. Stevenson High School is a suburban public school located in Lincolnshire, Illinois, in the northern suburbs of Chicago. In 2006, the school had just over 4,500 students, with a student-to-teacher ratio of 18.2 to 1 and a per-pupil expenditure of $11,981.

Stevenson's music program has four full-time and three part-time music teachers, one of whom is Clark Chaffee, director of orchestras and guitar instruction, who submitted the program to MENC. Within the Music Department, performance-based classes range from thirty to eighty students in size, while nonperformance classes range in size from twelve to twenty-four students. The total enrollment in all music courses is approximately 750 students, representing more than 16 percent of the student body. The 2006–2007 enrollment includes 315 students in band, 200 students in choir, and 135 students in orchestra.

Budget and Other Funding

The school board budget provides for equipment, materials, and operating expenses for the Music Department totaling about $220 per student (excluding salaries and stipends). Other covered expenses—though not included in the Music Department's budget—include postage, photocopying, and other similar expenses.

The band, choir, and orchestra programs each have active parent booster organizations that provide valuable assistance to faculty with special activities and projects, such as educational enrichment activities, social events, and travel. These groups also raise funds for their respective programs and the department as a whole.

These groups contribute in excess of $20,000 annually to the Music Department's activities, equipment, and uniform needs. The school budget, combined with this and other funding, meets the basic needs of Stevenson's music program.

Scheduling

At Stevenson, band, orchestra, choirs, guitar, and Advanced Placement Music Theory meet daily for fifty minutes throughout the school year. Composing and Arranging, Beginning Piano, and Discover Music (a secondary general music course), meet daily for fifty minutes for one semester. Discover Music includes beginning piano skills, elementary music theory, the study—through listening—of many styles and genres of music, and exploration of music technology, as well as some basic composition projects. Beginning Classical Guitar Technique is a two-semester class that applies classical guitar techniques and musicianship training to classical, pop, rock, blues, and folk repertoires.

Stevenson has five bands: freshman band, concert band, symphonic band, advanced symphonic band, and honor band. Each meets for fifty minutes daily. The school also has two orchestra levels: concert orchestra (three classes meet under this title) and patriot orchestra (the top ensemble). The following five choirs comprise Stevenson's choral program: three sections of the Stevenson chorus, advanced choir, and patriot singers (the top mixed ensemble).

The orchestras and choirs perform concerts in October, December, April, and May. All bands are involved in noncompetitive marching band in the fall, performing at home football games and in a local parade. All five bands present formal concerts in December, February, and April. In addition to these, each area annually sponsors a concert with sender schools. These "consortium concerts" create a collaborative environment where prospective future musi-

Choral students at Adlai E. Stevenson High School rehearse.

cians work alongside their high school counterparts. Band, choir, and orchestra students have the opportunity to participate in solo and ensemble contests and state and district honors ensembles. First- and second-tier groups also participate in concert and sight-reading contests. Each fall, Stevenson puts on a full-production school musical with strong band, orchestra, and choir involvement.

Music students can choose from the following menu of after-school cocurricular programs: five jazz/pop vocal groups, two jazz bands, and the Guitar Club. Upper-level band members also are assigned to play in the basketball pep band.

Music Facilities and Equipment

Stevenson's new $2 million orchestra and guitar rehearsal space has just been completed. The band room seats eighty students, the choir room seats forty students, and the orchestra room seats forty to sixty students. The school also has twelve practice rooms that seat two to six people each. They are used for private practice, small ensembles, private lessons, and small sectionals.

Stevenson's primary performance area is the Performing Arts Center, which consists of three spaces: a 700-seat main auditorium, a 250-seat recital hall, and a 250-seat little theater. The seats for the both the theater and the recital hall are on large turntables and can be turned to face the main auditorium stage, creating a 1,200-seat capacity for the main-stage audience. The construction of the turntable seating provides acoustic isolation, which allows for operating all three venues at the same time. Performance acoustics are excellent in all areas.

One other outstanding feature of the Stevenson Music Department is a twenty-five-station MIDI lab with current iMac computers, Yamaha synthesizers, up-to-date software, and an interactive lab monitoring system for communication between teacher and students. Students in all performance-based classes complete music theory–related assignments in the MIDI lab. The nonperformance courses meet in the lab daily as their primary classroom.

Sufficient funding has allowed Stevenson to make school instruments available for student use. These include the more expensive band instruments, as well as in-class instruments for orchestra (viola, cello, and bass) and guitar. Music teachers train students to take proper care of instruments, and replacement and repair is generally done as needed and is covered in the department budget. The music program has an extra set of large percussion instruments for the main stage of the Performing Arts Center. The choir room has a grand piano, as does the main stage. The recital hall and the little theater have upright pianos. Most of the practice rooms have either acoustic upright or eighty-eight-key electric pianos. The department also is outfitted with a sufficient quantity of high-quality music stands and chairs. Band and orchestra students also are provided individual instrument storage lockers within the department.

Music facility and equipment planning over the years has been helped greatly by referring to recommendations found in the MENC publication *Opportunity-to-Learn Standards for Music Instruction: PreK–12*, which has provided valuable guidelines and standards.

Philosophy of Music Education

Throughout Stevenson's Fine Arts Department, the faculty endeavors to warmly welcome all students who wish to enroll in music classes. The department also reflects the high expectations held by the community, school board, and administration.

The school's coursebook carries this statement, which reflects the department's identification with MENC:

> Music study provides unique opportunities for creativity and self-expression and promotes artistic and cultural awareness. It helps students develop skills in listening, awareness, teamwork, logical reasoning, problem solving, conceptualizing and communicating. The Stevenson Music Department offers a variety of classes that allow students to continue—or begin—a strong, sequential program of vocal and/or instrumental music study.

The Music Department embraces its role in preparing students to become active, lifelong music makers and leaders in professional and community music and music education. Those in Stevenson's music program believe that students must have comprehensive training in musical knowledge, technique, and musicianship, as well as a wide variety of performance opportunities with a broad range of repertoire.

Unique Aspects of the Program

Stevenson is a model professional learning community, and as such, the administration fosters a focus on collaborative work in and among curriculum teams. Each week, faculty teams are provided time to meet to set goals for student achievement; share materials, ideas, and techniques for instructional strategies; work on developing formative and summative assessment tools; evaluate data from tests and exams; and reflect on the effectiveness of their teaching. It is during these weekly collaborative meetings that the music faculty reviews the department's curriculum and how it addresses—or could better address—the MENC National Standards. This time for reflection and collaboration has resulted in a continuously evolving and improving curriculum, as well as continuous improvement in individual teaching.

The members of the music faculty see themselves as a single music faculty rather than independent band, orchestra, and choir divisions. Music students have many opportunities to support and collaborate with their peers in other ensembles, and classes offered throughout the department encourage students to explore opportunities for musical growth.

The music program's ensemble instructional strategy depends heavily upon team teaching. The school supports staffing that allows for assigning two certified teachers to each performance ensemble class (some of these assistant directors are compensated on a part-time basis). This approach allows one teacher to lead rehearsal while the partnering teacher conducts section-based, pull-out rehearsals or works with individuals or small groups for either instructional or assessment activities. Teacher partners share insights about individual and group progress, collaborate on lesson planning, and share conducting responsibilities.

At Stevenson, all performance classes have a rigorous music theory component that challenges students. Composition projects comprise part of the curriculum for the band, orchestra, and guitar programs. Many graduates of the program continue to compose at the university level. The school also has commissioned several pieces from professional composers and provides students the opportunity to interact with visiting composers.

Chamber music is central to Stevenson's music program. The instrumental faculty believes that chamber music experiences build individual musicianship as well as a deeper understanding of the importance of individual technical preparation. In 2007, the school's annual orchestra chamber festival saw 140 students perform in 35 ensembles. Orchestra chamber groups routinely give more than twenty performances annually at various school and community events. Ample funding for outside coaches supports the orchestral chamber music program. All students in the top two bands are assigned to small ensembles and in a six-week project are provided weekly release time from ensemble rehearsals to prepare for a formal chamber music recital.

All instrumental and vocal students are encouraged to participate in private lessons. The program provides them with easy access to private instruction with highly qualified professional musicians during the school day.

Latest Developments

Being recognized as a Model Music Program has enhanced the status of the Music Department within the school and in the larger community. It has prompted faculty to review how they present the program to the community and the broader public. Topics being examined include website enhancements, outreach activities, and ways to share teaching experiences and ideas with other educators.

Adlai E. Stevenson High School has a strong record as a national leader in secondary education. The U.S. Department of Education cited the quality of Stevenson fine arts programs as an important part of the reason the school received its fourth Blue Ribbon Award for Excellence in Education in 2002.

Recent initiatives include: beginning a Tri-M chapter; exploring and adopting "sister" orchestra programs in Chicago, New Orleans, and Mexico for purposes of student and educator interactions and growth; engaging administration in discussions about expanding guitar class offerings; and expanding American String Teachers Association chapter activities.

A task force of teachers, counselors, and administrators was assembled this year to examine the ways in which the school can better encourage its students to take advantage of a remarkable range of elective offerings in fine arts and other departments. There is a commitment to communicating effectively to students and parents the value of including elective courses in order to enrich and strengthen each student's high school education. The research and work this group is doing is certain to lead to growth in enrollment, as well as a continued, deepened commitment to support of the fine arts at Adlai E. Stevenson High School.

RUTLAND CITY PUBLIC SCHOOLS

Basic School District Description

Rutland City Public Schools serve 2,959 students in rural Vermont. Two K–2 buildings and an ungraded K–2 learning center, one building for grades 3–6, one middle school, and one high school make up the district. The average per-pupil expenditure is $7,662.

Budget and Other Funding

In the Rutland City Public Schools, the elementary, middle, and high schools share a budget of $12,000 to purchase instruments and $22,000 for stipends. Separate from this amount, the elementary schools receive $1,200 for maintenance, $500 for an accompanist, $750 for travel, $2,200 for supplies, $6,500 for books and music, $650 for equipment, and $750 for dues and fees. The middle school choral program receives $4,500 for an accompanist, $250 for maintenance, $1,200 for books and music, and $300 for dues and fees. The middle school band and orchestra program share a maintenance budget of

$1,200. In addition to this amount, the band program receives $1,000 for books and music, $250 for equipment, and $300 for dues and fees. The orchestra receives $1,200 for books and music and $300 for dues and fees.

At the high school level, the choral, band, and orchestra programs share a budget of $4,000 allocated for dues and fees and $2,800 for transportation. Additionally, the choral program receives $4,000 for an accompanist, $115 for other services, $250 for maintenance, $200 for supplies, and $1,500 for books and music.

The band program receives $600 for uniform cleaning, $1,000 for maintenance, $500 for travel, $500 for supplies, and $100 for audio and visual needs. The high school orchestra receives $350 for maintenance, $580 for transportation, $200 for travel, $200 for supplies, $1,000 for books and music, $100 for equipment, and $5,000 for a technical center for jazz and contemporary music (this is discussed later in detail).

Other funding includes the Stoolfire Fund of $5,000–$10,000, depending on the market. The Stoolfire Fund is a trust fund bequeathed by a Rutland City citizen to the public schools that stipulates that the yearly interest is to be used for the Music Department only. The fund cannot go toward the purchase of instruments, however, as the donor believed that is the responsibility of the school board and citizens. It does go toward upgrading sound systems in every music classroom, computers, visiting artists, and fees for use of the community's theater.

Additionally, parent groups, students, and ensembles raise money for a major trip every other year, and a trip to Florida every four years. Together these groups raise $20,000–$40,000.

Scheduling

In the elementary schools of Rutland City, K–2 students have a music class each week for thirty-five minutes. Students in grades 3–6 have general music for forty minutes weekly. Students in grades 3–4 participate in ensembles that meet for forty-five minutes every day. Four ensembles are available to these students: beginning orchestra, beginning band (fourth grade only), intermediate orchestra, and choral experience. Students in grades 5–6 participate in ensembles that meet for forty-five minutes every day. Six ensembles are available to these students: beginning band, beginning orchestra, intermediate band, advanced band, advanced orchestra, and chorus.

In the middle school, seventh- and eighth-grade students are required to take general music and have an hour-long class daily for a fifth of the school year. The school also has what they call an *experiential* block for the first hour every day. During this time, the school offers orchestra, seventh-grade chorus, eighth-grade chorus, and concert band. Before school, the middle school has a lab jazz ensemble (open to all instruments) that meets twice per week and a select choral group that meets after school twice per week. The directors receive stipends for leading these groups.

At the high school, every freshman is required to take the school's fine arts survey course for half of a credit. Team-taught by music, visual art, and theater teachers, it fulfills half of the one-credit fine arts requirement for graduation. The high school offers two bands, two choruses, an orchestra, two levels of jazz ensemble, a select singing group, and general music and theory courses during the school day. Performing courses are for the entire year, and the others are for half of the year. Outside of the academic day, the high school offers a pep band, a male a cappella singing group, a choral festival preparation group, and Tri-M. Instructors of all of these groups receive stipends.

Music Facilities and Equipment

The band program has full percussion in grades 3–12, though only the middle and high schools have vibraphones. The schools provide students in grades 4–12 with oboes, bassoons, larger clarinets, French horns, tubas, and larger saxophone synthesizers. Classrooms have instrument storage lockers and podiums. Rutland City Schools also have budgeted a $12,000 replacement program in which they can replace band and orchestra instruments.

In the orchestra program, classrooms have percussion equipment, cellos, and basses (the school attempts to provide two basses per player for home and school use). A limited number of violins and violas are available for students with financial need who desire to play one of these instruments rather than cello or bass.

The two primary buildings (grades K–2) have a new music/art room with a piano and stereo system and ample room for movement exercises. The intermediate school (grades 3–6) has a vocal room, an orchestral music room, and a music/art room, all equipped with pianos and sound systems and spacious enough for large instrumental ensemble rehearsals. Rutland has one shared theater (used throughout the day as an additional ensemble space) with great acoustics, seating for five hundred people, and a complete sound system. In addition, there is one shared music room attached to the middle school. The middle school has a tiered music room with a complete sound system, a new piano, the district's instrument repair shop, and a practice room.

The high school has a recital and theater hall that allows for various setups. This room is used as a rehearsal space for the orchestra and one of the jazz ensembles. The high school also has a chorus room with two practice rooms and a band/orchestra room with practice and storage rooms. Each space has a complete sound, recording, and playback system. The choral classrooms have extensive libraries and pianos in good repair at all levels.

Philosophy of Music Education

Rutland Public Schools have the following fine arts vision statement: "We educate the students of Rutland City Schools to be active and knowledgeable consumers of the arts, who will engage in lifelong involvement in the arts, and will respect and appreciate beauty and sensitivity."

Prior to 1993, music had been cut from kindergarten completely and reduced to once weekly for half a year for grades 1–6. In 1997, the Music Department rewrote the current philosophy to protect elementary music instruction in the future.

Those who teach the music curriculum believe that music is worth knowing and that schools have an obligation to transmit cultural heritage as expressed through music to succeeding generations as well as to help each student develop his or her musical potential. Believing that music provides an outlet for creativity and self-expression, the program promotes the study of music to help students understand the nature of humankind.

Unique Aspects of the Program

Rutland City Schools considers their technical center program as the most unique aspect of their program. This program attracts serious drum, keyboard, guitar, and bass players—a student population often overlooked in traditional programs. At the technical center, students can study jazz and contemporary music intensively for one or two years and earn advanced college credit at some area colleges. Other unique aspects include the opportunity for students as young as third grade to participate in ensembles.

In addition to ensembles, Rutland City Schools has mandatory music instruction for grades K–9. At the high school, all freshman must take a fine arts survey course, The Arts: Where Do You Fit In? Faculty believes this course leads students to make better-informed choices when selecting the other fine arts half credit required for graduation.

The Rutland community has made a large investment in the arts, especially music. The state of Vermont made a funding change favorable to the city, which chose to strengthen the arts. Those in Rutland are proud of the small city's commitment to the arts.

Latest Developments

Rutland Public Schools have recently adjusted the elementary performance program. All ensembles now meet daily Monday through Thursday; Friday is set aside for instrumental lessons. The district continues to have strong support from the community and has a new initiative to replace its aging piano inventory.

NANUET UNION FREE SCHOOL DISTRICT

Basic District Description

Located in a suburb of New York City, Nanuet Union Free School District consists of four schools: George Miller Elementary School (K–3), Highview Elementary School (4–5), A. MacArthur Barr Middle School (6–8), and Nanuet Senior High School (9–12). The district serves 2,298 students and has a student-to-teacher ratio of 10 to 1. The music program has one part-time and eleven full-time music teachers, and 90 percent of students participate in music classes. The per-pupil expenditure is $16,025.

Budget and Other Funding

The music budget is districtwide and controlled directly by the director of music, Dr. Jack Gremli, who submitted Nanuet's program to MENC. The total music budget, excluding salaries, is $66,679. From this amount, the district allocates $10,025 for equipment, $6,500 for repairs, $20,000 for plays and musicals, $12,000 for the New York State School Music Association, $1,000 for textbooks, $16,154 for instructional supplies, and $1,000 for district dues.

Nanuet's only outside source of funding comes from the Nanuet Music Parents Association, which grants scholarships and awards merchandise to the

department. For example, the organization awards $3,000 annually to gradu-
ating seniors for their future studies in the performing arts. Monetary awards
totaling $2,000 are given to underclassmen for private study. Merchandise has
taken the form of Broadway show tickets, New York Philharmonic concert
tickets, opera tickets, Jazz at Lincoln Center tickets, and so on.

Scheduling

At the elementary schools, all class periods are forty-five minutes long unless otherwise noted. Kindergarten and first graders have one music class per
six-day cycle. Second graders have two classes per six-day cycle, consisting of
one general music class and one violin class. Third graders have one class per
six-day cycle, which includes recorder and singing in addition to general music. They may also elect to continue in string class (which is either pull-out or
before school). All fourth and fifth graders have two classes per week, which
include general music and chorus, and students may elect band or orchestra.
Fourth- and fifth-grade bands and orchestras have one class per week as well
as one small-group lesson per week.

All middle school classes are forty-three minutes long unless noted otherwise. Each middle school student has one music class every other day for
twenty weeks in every grade. Sixth-grade chorus meets once every four days
and is mandatory. Sixth-grade band and orchestra are electives and meet once
every other day, and students also have one small-group lesson per week. In
seventh grade, chorus is an elective for the first time, and the seventh- and
eighth-grade choruses meet every other day. There is a combined seventh-
and eighth-grade band that meets once every other day, plus one small-group
lesson per week. A combined seventh- and eighth-grade orchestra also has one
class every other day, plus one small-group lesson per week. Jazz band, chamber orchestra, and concert choir meet for fifty minutes after school once per
week. Scheduling allows for participation in more than one ensemble. Teachers are paid a stipend for leading after-school ensembles.

At the high school level, classes are forty-three minutes long unless otherwise noted. Music Theory and Advanced Placement Music Theory have one
class every day. Band has one class daily and one small-group lesson per week.
Jazz band has two classes weekly. The mixed chorus and concert choir have
one class daily. Orchestra has one class daily plus one small-group lesson per
week. The symphonic orchestra and chamber orchestra have one class each

per week. Music independent study sessions take place twice per week. Like the middle school, scheduling allows for participation in more than one ensemble.

Applied Music gives high school students credit for private lessons taken outside of school. Music Technology is one fifty-minute class after school weekly. The high school has a performing arts council (the music student governing body), which meets after school for thirty minutes weekly. The Music and Performing Arts Departments put on a fall play and spring musical.

Music Facilities and Equipment

The band program has a full array of wind and percussion instruments that double those kept at home by students. When a student provides proof of rental or purchase of the "home-based" instrument, he or she receives a school-owned instrument for use at school. If a family cannot afford to rent or purchase a home instrument, the student receives a second school-owned instrument.

Band classrooms have ample chairs and music stands, audio equipment for recording and playback, four computers plus one in the teacher office, lockable storage cabinets for all student and school-owned instruments, an acoustic piano, an electric digital keyboard, and a music library system.

The orchestras have a full array of large string instruments to double those kept at home by students. Orchestra classrooms have ample chairs and music stands, audio equipment for recording and playback, four computers plus one in the teacher office, lockable storage cabinets for all student and school-owned instruments, an acoustic piano, an electric digital keyboard, and a music library system.

Choral programs have two acoustic pianos and one digital piano. Classrooms have choral risers, Wenger chairs, music stands, a music library system, and audio equipment for amplification, recording, and playback.

In addition to the band, orchestra, and choral facilities, Highview Elementary has a fully outfitted music technology lab. Five stations contain musical keyboards connected by MIDI cables to Dell hardware. Music Ace and Finale constitute the main music software used. Barr Middle School has fifteen stations equipped similarly to Highview but also has custom-designed iMac stations. At the high school, a soundproof room contains two stations with keyboards and Macintosh computers, two sequencing

*In the Nanuet Union Free School District, two eighth-grade bassists per-
form in concert.*

keyboards, and two television monitors. The room also contains a practice room that doubles as a recording space.

Philosophy of Music Education

The Nanuet Union Free School District holds the philosophy that music constitutes an academic area equal in opportunity and responsibility to all other academic areas in the district. Like all other content areas, music has a comprehensive curriculum design for kindergarten through twelfth grade, continuing professional development opportunities, objective and subjective reporting of student progress, and, in the middle and high school, inclusion of course grades for honors and class ranking consideration.

Unique Aspects of the Program

Although the New York State Regents requirements have greatly increased during the last ten years and No Child Left Behind has caused many reductions and, in many cases, destruction of arts programs nationwide, the Nanuet Union Free School District has maintained its commitment to music as an essential part of every student's education. The music program has seen an increase in its staff, department budget, and curricular and cocurricular offerings. The attrition percentage of elective participation has held steady or decreased.

Every high school student is made aware of his or her learning style and strengths by completing the Dunn and Dunn Learning Styles Inventory. Teachers learn their students' strengths and adjust classroom practices to accommodate their learning style preferences and ensure differentiated instruction.

Nanuet has several unique programs, such as the second-grade string program, elementary and intermediate interdisciplinary enrichment programs, composition curriculum in the middle school general music program, and the "Amby" awards given to the outstanding recordings of the eighth-grade compositions. The middle school has an opera program connected with the Metropolitan Opera Guild that exposes forty-four students annually to the art form.

At the high school level, the comprehensive choral program addresses four aspects of the choral curriculum in a unique way. Four areas of vocal technique—music history, composer biography, music theory, and artistic expression—are used to generate thematic exploration that culminates in a theme-based concert. Scientifically determined student learning style strengths guide instruction and assessment. The curriculum is based on the thought that "the more one knows the better one performs"—a truly comprehensive approach to the performing arts.

Student compositions are performed regularly in class, at concerts, and as incidental music for dramatic productions, and a composer-in-residence teaches composition in the middle school. The performing arts council serves as the student organization responsible for Music Department policy and is the nucleus of the Nanuet chapter of Tri-M. Not limited to the school year, the Nanuet summer music program keeps more than one hundred student musicians practicing, performing, and learning every summer.

The *New York Times* has named the Music Department in the Nanuet Union Free School District as one of the main reasons families move to the community. Nothing happens in the Nanuet Union Free School District without music—it accompanies every orientation, tribute to retiring staff, and display of appreciation for the PTA.

Latest Developments

Since its recognition as a Model Music Program, construction in all four buildings has improved the music areas of each building. Nanuet restructured its schools' grade levels, which resulted in more rehearsal time for all performing ensembles in the middle school and continued to allow students to take part in multiple performing groups.

The Opera Club at the middle school has grown to more than sixty regular participants. The advisor of the Opera Club (who writes lesson plans for the Metropolitan Opera Guild) and members of the Opera Club have appeared as intermission guests on satellite radio broadcasts live from the Metropolitan Opera House.

Representatives of the Ministry of Education from Singapore visited the Nanuet Union Free School District at the suggestion of Grant Wiggins, author of the "Understanding by Design" (UbD) curriculum model. The high school concert choir class demonstrated how UbD could be applied to the classroom setting. The question posed for the demonstration class was "What does excellence in performance look and sound like?"

The "Song of the Year" from the eighth-grade general music songwriting curriculum was broadcast live and streamed internationally on WVBR, Cornell University's radio station, as a part of its up-and-coming new artists series. The song was written and recorded on the equipment purchased with funds from the Model Music Program Grant.

Since its recognition as a Model Music Program, the American Music Council named Nanuet one of the one hundred best communities in America for music education. Finally, the total music budget has increased to fit the needs of the ever-expanding music program.

DISCUSSION

Most music educators agree that they need not include every standard in each class or lesson plan but that they do need to make sure they adequately integrate each standard by the end of the course or semester. Developing a standards-based curriculum becomes much more manageable when the National Standards are used as a structure for curriculum rather than, say, a rubric for how good or bad a program is.

The programs in the Rutland City Public Schools, in Nanuet, and at Adlai E. Stevenson articulate a standards-based curriculum through the structure of their programs. For example, Rutland has mandatory music study for students in grades K–9, and students in fifth and sixth grade have the opportunity to participate in instrumental music. The district also has a strong middle school program in which all students take general music and have the option of participating in an ensemble as well.

Lesson plans for Rutland reflect attention to standards at all levels. Kindergarten students might have a lesson in pitch exploration that addresses National Standards 1, 3, and 5. Ninth-grade students in the arts survey course—technically not an "official" music course—will learn material related to Standards 2, 3, 4, 5, and 7 as they determine which of the fine arts most attracts them.

Like Rutland schools, music programs in Nanuet also highly value elementary music education. Its second-grade strings program most obviously exemplifies this. In addition to a strong elementary program, Nanuet strives to maintain comprehensive, standards-based music education up into the high school. The choral program, for example, examines in-depth music theory, composer biography and milieu, and artistic expression for a theme-based concert, based on the idea that students will perform better when they simply know *more* about what they are performing.

Adlai E. Stevenson High School is the only single-school program in this chapter. Stevenson integrates the National Standards in many ways and has a useful way of demonstrating the distribution of and degree to which standards are addressed by using a simple table (see table 4.1). Other programs can replicate this table with their own courses to evaluate their programs' alignment with the National Standards.

Stevenson's table shows the music faculty that every music course addresses at least six standards. These courses, many of which are common to most high schools, integrate the standards in unique yet imitable ways. For example, Advanced Placement Music Theory includes daily sight singing. Students in this class are also frequently listening to and learning about examples of music from a wide variety of historical periods and cultures.

Bands, orchestras, and choirs all have a considerable amount of music theory (including harmony) incorporated into their multitiered curricula, as well as a composition project for all students who are in their ensemble's most advanced curriculum. Orchestra rehearsals often include students singing passages to help internalize interpretation and style as well as pitch to improve intonation. They also learn basics of blues improvisation and harmony. The choir faculty provides background sheets on class repertoire that provide information about the song's cultural and historical context as well as its unique compositional elements.

The secondary general music course, Discover Music, has beginning piano skills as a primary focus. This reflects the faculty's belief that students who truly wish to learn about music need to learn how to read and perform music as opposed to simply listening to and discussing it.

The beginning classical guitar curriculum initiates the development of classical guitar technique and comprehensive musicianship. Students learn to read pitch (standard notation and TAB), rhythm, and chord notation. Assignments include learning key signatures and scale patterns, improvising, performing of classical guitar solo and ensemble repertoire, singing, playing/transposing folk songs, and creating accompaniment patterns, bass lines, and harmonies. Many of the assignments incorporate the use of the blues scale and progression. Composing is an important part of second-semester activities. Beginning piano

Table 4.1. Integration of National Standards in the Adlai E. Stevenson High School Music Program

National Standard	Bands	Choirs	Orchestra	Advanced Placement Music Theory	Discover Music	Composing and Arranging	Piano	Guitar
1. Singing	1	2	1	0	0	0	0	1
2. Playing	2	0	2	1	2	1	2	2
3. Improvising	0	0	1	0	1	1	1	1
4. Composing/Arranging	1	1	2	2	1	2	0	2
5. Read/Notate Music	2	2	2	2	2	2	2	2
6. Listen and Analyze	2	2	1	2	2	1	0	1
7. Evaluate Performances	2	2	1	2	2	1	2	0
8. Music Relationships	0	1	0	2	2	1	1	0
9. Historical and Cultural	1	2	1	2	2	1	0	0

The National Standard is 2–often addressed, 1–sometimes addressed, 0–not addressed students also study music theory and build skills necessary to compose and improvise.

The Composing and Arranging class frequently involves listening to music in a wide variety of styles and genres, followed by an analysis of characteristic compositional elements. This study leads to assignments in creating compositions and arrangements in various styles and for a variety of ensembles.

To address understanding music in relation to history and culture, a project is being developed in which music students will prepare and present Internet research projects.

Importantly, Stevenson continuously reviews the curriculum in relation to the National Standards, and faculty addresses those areas that it feels need to be more fully incorporated into the curriculum.

Like all of the Model Music Programs, these three programs' per-pupil expenditure varies widely, from $7,662 in rural Vermont to $11,981 in a Midwestern suburb to $16,025 in a suburb near New York City. Perhaps more than any other focus area in this book, however, standards-based education is least dependent upon budget. All three programs have community and administrative support; communities value their music programs, and the administration supports maintaining standards that reflect music's rightful place as a core academic subject.

5

The Big Picture

Music educators have long been interested and involved in the collection of model ideas from the field. In periodicals, books, discussions and presentations at meetings and conventions, and online communications, the identification and promulgation of models have been how the profession—often through the efforts of MENC: The National Association for Music Education—has moved forward. And both preservice and in-service education of teachers involves the study of such models as the basis for practice.

Lack of models is rarely a problem for a teacher or supervisor searching for ideas to improve the ways that music programs serve students; however, that same teacher or supervisor may find the study of models inspiring but of limited utility. After all, each of the fifteen thousand or so school systems in the United States, and often each of the many schools within those districts, faces a different set of advantages and limitations in adopting new practices, even if those practices have proven stunningly effective in a different context. Individual schools and individual teachers within those schools have different strengths and talents that they can bring to bear on educational issues, and those strengths and talents may not match those that form the basis of success for the teacher at the core of a model in a different school or class.

Since the development of the National Standards for Music Education in 1994, music teachers and supervisors have at least had a consensus framework within which to judge outcomes, so the idea of what constitutes a "model" program may be somewhat more than a platonic ideal. But teachers and supervisors really need ideas on ways to interpret model programs, ways to sort through the many available models and select from those models key elements that need to be studied, replicated, and adapted for the systems in which they try to serve students.

The stakes are high for teachers' professional outlooks, as educators are always oriented toward the achievement of the students in their charge. And increasingly, as the music education profession moves to more sophisticated models for program assessment and as community expectations for program outcomes continue to rise, the stakes are high on a social and political scale, as well. Professional music educators need not only increased communication about relevant models but also more information on the ways in which those models can be replicated in disparate schools and communities around the nation. Without the ability to be accountable to communities for the quality of education in our music programs, and without the ability to articulate the ways that those music programs are moving toward acknowledged models of effectiveness, music programs may be in an increasingly precarious position.

FINDING AND ANALYZING MODELS

Key to the usefulness of model programs for education is an analysis of the aspects that make them models and some ideas as to how those models can be replicated around the nation. After all, in a nation where some 50 million children are served in some 100,000 public schools (not to mention thousands of private and parochial schools), celebrating the unique efforts of a few gifted educators or an enlightened administration here or there is simply not enough. If we are to spread the benefits of high-quality music education to *all* American children, we need to look for factors that go beyond local idiosyncrasies to factors that can provide practical focus for improvement of programs in schools across the nation.

There are, of course, limitations to this approach to identifying models and the characteristics that might drive or define those models. For example, the determination of which programs were to be named as "models" was made by representatives of the music education profession, not by reference to characteristics defined by an outside, independent body. First, the 156 submissions to the program were self-selected by educators in the field as worthy of model status—and those educators certainly applied what they considered to be the prevailing standards of what constitutes a model before deciding whether they were going to make the significant outlay in time and effort to submit their programs. Next, the panel of educators who rated the programs, selecting the top programs, used their many years of experience as music educators to determine which programs met prevailing standards of excellence. Those educators were working in the context of the 1994 National Standards for Music Education, which list the knowledge and skills that should be imparted by music programs. They were also working with an evaluation rubric that emphasized four factors:

1. Educational standards
2. Replicability
3. Originality
4. System dependability

The thrust of these factors was an attempt to seek out programs that rely on the strength of structure and resources rather than the strength of a specific leader's personality or character, so that elements of the programs are likely to be useful in other situations.

Analysis of the model programs in this project yields five major factors that seem to be present in all or almost all cases. The Model Music Programs reflect these five characteristics that other educators might examine to improve their own programs, though no list can adequately describe the depth or complexity of any program. These characteristics are:

1. Adequate resources
2. Universality
3. Exemplary personnel
4. Strong community ties
5. Clear creative vision

CHARACTERISTIC 1: ADEQUATE RESOURCES

What is an "adequate" level of resources? Some of this—particularly funding levels—will doubtless vary by community as costs of goods and services vary by community. Guidelines for determining what constitutes adequate resources might best be done by calculating the funds necessary to meet the Opportunity-to-Learn Standards for Music Instruction, published in 1994 and available on the MENC website at www.menc.org/publication/books/otl.html.

Funds

Exact amounts of funding that support model programs vary widely by the nature of the program and the geographic area in which the program functions. On average, the programs selected as models worked in systems with slightly higher per-pupil expenditures than did other submitted programs, but the differences were not overwhelming. The nature of funding sources varies as well: some programs have independent budgets, and some are funded on an "as needed" basis by the building principal or other supervisor; some do extensive outside fund-raising, while others do not. But while funding is not by itself sufficient to make for a model program, each of the programs listed reported at least adequate funding that is not overly dependent on outside sources. One submission reported, "I have been told to write more grants, instead of fund-raising. The kids do some kind of fund-raising monthly, and I was advised against doing another."

Time

Again, this is somewhat variable depending on the courses used to deliver knowledge and skills to students, but serious curricular goals need serious instructional time. Programs designated as models had slightly more instructional time than did other submissions (at the elementary level, an average of sixty-nine minutes per week as opposed to an average of sixty-five minutes per week), but all programs submitted shared in this essential commitment to providing instruction to students in music.

Facilities

All the model programs had facilities that were, while not always ideal, at least sufficient for the needs of the program. These facilities ranged from new rehearsal spaces to things as basic as a sufficient number of music stands.

Stability

This is a factor that truly stood out in the programs studied and one that is not specifically addressed in the Opportunity-to-Learn Standards. The model programs described in the project share more than the fact that they can draw on adequate resources for the year in which they described their programs—they share in the presence of a prolonged commitment to adequate resources on the part of decision makers. One model program submission defined this as "systematic stability in the music program," leading to a "culture of excellence." This allows programs to grow into systems that can truly serve students with comprehensive, sequential, substantive music experiences, even when faced by the structural challenges that come with demographic shifts, scheduling changes, and other realities of the public schools. The ways that this is done varies: one submission reported that "music was kept as an indispensable part of the school's education program when we went to an A/B block schedule with 90 minute periods ten years ago. A member of the music staff served on the scheduling/curriculum revision committee."

CHARACTERISTIC 2: UNIVERSALITY

The programs named as model programs—and the majority of those submitted as models—shared a concern with reaching all or at least most of the students in their schools or school districts. For model districtwide programs, some 77 percent of students were involved; at the school level, programs awarded model status reached 81 percent participation. Even where programs cited select ensembles or other programs that served relatively small numbers of students electing specific high school courses, these programs were built as part of programs that at earlier grade levels reached out to the vast majority of students. This seems to serve both a philosophical ideal (music for all students) and a practical one: where all students are given a good basis in music, more will discover that they have the aptitude and interest needed for deeper elective study. One program reported,

> We teach general music to all students in grades K–6 thirty minutes once a week. Band starts in fifth grade, and I traditionally start over 50 percent of the grade in band. Our music program includes General Music in grades K–6; Music Appreciation in ninth grade, which includes a unit on guitar; and Beginning

Band, Intermediate Band, Marching Band and Concert Band scheduled during the school day. After-school programs include: Jazz Band, String Class, and Private Lessons. We have a competitive band program, which consistently receives superior ratings, and individually, my students place highly in district/state honor bands and solo and ensemble competitions. We have a chapter of Tri-M Music Honor Society. My goal is to help them develop a lifelong love of music.

Even in the case of a model program at a magnet school, the program submission includes the report that "throughout the school's fine arts department, there is a respect for the fact that we are a public school. We warmly welcome all students who wish to enroll."

CHARACTERISTIC 3: EXEMPLARY PERSONNEL

Staff Numbers

The model programs submitted all had sufficient highly motivated, well-educated staff to meet the educational goals of the programs. In addition, levels of staffing and levels of motivation worked together: while some teacher schedules described in submissions seem to impose burdens that might go beyond what could be considered reasonable, the teachers involved seemed concerned only about their ability to reach the students. That said, the pupil–teacher ratios of those selected as model programs were, on the average, lower than those not named as models (thirteen pupils per teacher for those designated as models versus twenty for other submissions by school systems).

Cooperation from Other Faculty

Teachers in model programs often cited the cooperation of other faculty and, especially, the administration as a basis for success. One elementary-level submission sums up this factor quite nicely: "During concerts, a first and a fourth grade teacher accompany the chorus to enable the music teacher to conduct. During rehearsals, the music teacher accompanies the choruses. Outside of the school day, many students study with a private instructor in the community."

Highly Trained Faculty

Statistics show that music teachers are more likely to have specific training in their field than their colleagues in most other subjects. In addition, the programs submitted for consideration as models seemed to be taught by teachers with very high educational and artistic credentials. This is evidenced by the fact that some model programs mentioned the ongoing involvement of their faculty in performing organizations outside the school and ongoing efforts to use mentor systems and other approaches to continually improve staff quality. One program submission reported that

> the staff (performing artists as well as artists in the classroom) includes but is certainly not limited to a published music education researcher, a full-time composer-in-residence, a member of the executive board of the New York State Band Association, copresident of the County Music Educators Association, and an internationally renowned violinist.

CHARACTERISTIC 4: STRONG COMMUNITY TIES

Accountability

Model programs engage routinely and actively in activities that ensure accountability to the public by demonstrating the musical achievements of the students served by the programs. This is done through performances to the community and through adjudicated festivals or events (both for ensembles and for soloists drawn from those ensembles). The consistency with which model programs emphasized attention to this overt, public demonstration of program quality is especially interesting in comparison to other subject areas, where the primary indicators used for public accountability are tests that themselves are the subject of debate as to relevance in the educational goals of the program. The discipline of music, as taught in our schools, has long had truly public demonstrations of program quality, at least in that large segment of American music education that is the school performing ensemble. Even in the relatively new area of music composition in the schools, one program designated as a model noted the development of an eighth-grade songwriting "competition" culminating in an awards ceremony that "has become a highlight of the school year."

Participation

Model programs see themselves as part of the school community and of the community served by the school. This is especially interesting with regard to current debates over the importance of integrating all aspects of a given student's educational experience (National Center on Education and the

Economy 2006); it appears from both the programs selected as models and all those self-selected for submission that music programs are now and have been for some time aware of the importance of serving the greater educational community while targeting subject-specific goals. Those programs designated as models do so to a high degree.

Using Resources

Model programs make full use of but are not driven by available artistic resources in the community and beyond. National programs used included those of Carnegie Hall, the New York Philharmonic, and the Metropolitan Opera. And these resources include, where available, ties to local performing organizations (especially local college or university performing organizations) and interdependence with local private studio teachers. Most importantly, however, the teachers and administrators involved in these programs believe the use of these resources is a true enhancement to the overall music education program.

CHARACTERISTIC 5: CLEAR CREATIVE VISION

Mission Focus

Each model program has a clear vision of the ways that the program fits in the overall educational mission of the school and the communities' aspirations for their children. One truly key, replicable factor in constructing a model program seems to be the adoption of a self-aware strategy for defining success, for achieving that success, and for analyzing progress toward that success on an ongoing basis. This planning task is certainly one that every teacher and supervisor can adopt in his or her work to build a true model program. Specifically, the programs designated as models uniformly referred to national and state standards, as well as to overall mission statements such as "to provide the most positive educational experience for all the children in our district."

Creativity

Each model program attempts to meet its vision through a truly remarkable set of creative solutions to the artistic, logistic, and educational challenges posed by diverse groups of students. While it can certainly be said that the educational strategies used all represent good practice, the breadth of that good practice matches the breadth of the musical experience itself. The programs designated as models used, to name a few strategies,

1. Band
2. String ensemble
3. Show choir
4. "Mozart Math"
5. Individual education programs
6. Native American flute instruction
7. Fiddling
8. Integrated music technologies
9. Drum circles
10. Keyboard
11. Music theory and composition
12. A five-week beginner instrumental program
13. Chamber music

CONCLUSION

The five characteristics described are all replicable—where the political will exists to replicate them. They are all scaleable, that is, they could all apply to both small, school-based programs and to larger systems that serve many schools and many thousands of students. And none of them are counter-intuitive; most teachers would agree that these are factors that must be pursued if school systems nationwide are to boast of "model" programs.

As a matter of fact, they share so much intuitive value that they might be called "the five painfully obvious characteristics of model programs." As is often the case in educational systems, good practice based on generations of experience by teachers, administrators, and community members may be worth considerably more than the latest ephemeral trend. These real model programs from real schools, if nothing else, make clear the value of good, obvious, educational practices.

So this list of model programs represents a selection of programs that meet the broadly drawn standards of the music education profession. As those standards have evolved in the context of communities and schools nationwide and as they include the formally adopted National Standards for Music Education, it is reasonable to believe that the standards applied to select these model programs are in line with community expectations for music programs. But our nation is in the midst of a continuing discussion over the desired outcomes for all educational programs. As that discussion continues to evolve, the consensus on what constitutes a model in a school music program may evolve as well.

These five characteristics need to be in place if we are to serve children with model programs. The characteristics can and should be used to analyze the basis on which individual programs are built. And these characteristics can and should be used to buttress local efforts to reform and strengthen programs.

These five characteristics don't constitute a silver bullet that will save music education. They do not point to defined methodologies, canons of musical literature, or set texts. Indeed, a cursory look at the programs listed would seem to rule out the definition of some set curriculum based on these models; the approaches submitted are simply too varied in the exact ways that they approach the process of delivering musical knowledge and skills to students. At the core, music teachers—and students—seem to be just too creative to warrant a "programmed learning" approach (see characteristic 5, "Creativity"). But these characteristics just may present a list of desirable factors that enable teachers, administrators, and communities to work together for the good of all our children.

The good news is that real-world models exist—so the attainment of that status is within the grasp of educators, supervisors, and communities everywhere.

6

Practical Applications

Submissions for the Model Music Program varied widely: Applications came from small individual schools and large school districts, from remote rural areas and from large suburban communities. Per-pupil expenditure ranged from approximately $5,000 to almost $20,000. The selected music programs demonstrate that successfully building and sustaining a model program relies on the combined hard work of teachers, administrators, parents, and the community at large. When all of these groups are involved, no matter the size, location, or budget, a music program can provide students with a vehicle for growth and creativity and become an asset to the community.

In addition to the work and planning of music education supporters, music programs require adequate and dependable resources, a goal of universality, exemplary personnel and collaboration among teachers, strong community ties, and a clear vision to make them paradigms of strong music programs. As discussed below, the Model Music Programs have much to share with us. In addition, MENC: The National Association for Music Education strives to support and inform music educators, and most of its Web content and magazine and journal articles are available without cost.

STRONG SUPPORT FROM THE ADMINISTRATION FOR MUSIC EDUCATION

All twelve winners of MENC's Model Music Program receive strong support for music education from administrators. All of them. All of the schools and districts selected consider music to be part of the basic core curriculum. For example, Nanuet Union Free School District (New York) believes that music is an academic area equal to all other academic areas. The winning programs also embrace the philosophy that music education should be available to all students. Page Middle School (Arizona) believes that everyone deserves a music education. East Ramapo Central School District (New York) has a committee to provide the opportunity for every student to study music. Its Music Department credits the success of the music program to the strong support received from the school administration, school board, and community, who all believe in the value of music participation for all students. The East Meadow School District (New York) hopes that their students' involvement in music will lead to a lifetime appreciation for music and skills that will carry over to other facets of their lives. Such attitudes from the school administration lead to strong music programs.

Music educators in less fortunate districts may ask "How can I get my administrators on board?" MENC is a national voice for music education and an authority on the issues of arts and education. In addition to consulting with congressional and federal agency offices on the importance of music education, on a practical level, MENC works to provide resources to assist teachers and supervisors in their music education advocacy efforts. MENC's website provides an assortment of resources, including advocacy webinars, in its "Advocacy Central" section (www.menc.org/advocacy/).

In its position statement "Advocacy and the Music Educator," MENC stresses that "every music educator needs to be a strong advocate for viable, sequential, enduring music programs for all students." There are many ways to advocate high-quality music education programs, and MENC's position statement discusses the music educator's role and detailed guidelines for starting an advocacy process. Some of the most effective ways to promote a music education program can be part of a music educator's regular activities: building and maintaining a strong, vital, quality music education program; using concerts and public performances to inform the audience of the content of the music being performed and the musical challenges students have met and mastered; and inviting an administrator into the music classroom or rehearsal to see students engaged in active learning. This informal form of advocacy can build support for the program and demonstrate the unique educational value of a music education.

In its position statement, "The Value and Quality of Arts Education," MENC emphasizes that every student should have an education in the arts and that the arts should be recognized as "serious, core academic subjects." The statement also discusses the correlation between arts education and improved SAT scores; research indicating that music instruction enhances the same higher brain functions required for mathematics, chess, science, and engineering; and findings that show the study of the arts teaches students how to work cooperatively, pose and solve problems, and develop higher-level thinking skills.

MENC publications frequently contain articles on advocacy. The August 2006 issue of *Teaching Music* has a special section on advocacy, "Sounding the Theme: Advocacy Programs Work for Us." In that special section are several articles on advocacy: "Speaking to Government about Music Education," which explains MENC's efforts and provides links to other organizations who help music advocates; "An Advocate for Advocacy," which spotlights an MENC member who is a leader in advocacy in Pennsylvania; and "Have Your Facts Ready!" which provides advice from an MENC member on dealing with government officials in defense of music education.

The *Music Educators Journal* has also tackled the issue of advocacy for music education. In the November 2004 issue, the article "Electing Music Advocates" points out that in many cases, school boards are elected or at least appointed by elected officials. When the League of Women Voters sought questions for candidates running for the local school board, music educators seized the opportunity to find out about the candidates' potential support for music education and to endorse "music friendly" candidates. The article also provides guidelines and some sample questions to put to those seeking elected office. In the same issue, the article "MENC Partners with Arts Groups to Advocate Music" describes arts groups that work to further the cause of music education. In the May 2004 issue, the article "Educate Our Advocates!" suggests one way to create educational opportunities for administrators, teachers, parents, and students designed to build a stronger foundation of support for what music educators do.

For specific facts on ancillary benefits of music education, myriad studies have found various benefits in music education. In the October 2006 issue of *Teaching Music*, the article "Principals Say Music Programs Affect

Graduation" reports on the results of a study released by MENC, NAMM (International Music Products Association), and the American Music Conference. The study found that the majority (96 percent) of principals interviewed agree that participating in music education encourages and motivates students to stay in school. Furthermore, 89 percent of principals believe a high-quality music education program contributes to higher graduation rates. Objective data back up these figures. Schools with music programs have significantly higher graduation rates than do those without programs (90.2 percent versus 72.9 percent) and have significantly higher attendance rates (93.3 percent versus 84.9 percent). More information on the study can be found in the special center insert in the February 2007 issue of *Teaching Music* and on the NAMM website at www.namm.org/wannaplay/public-attitudes.

MENC and other organizations have been active in accumulating information on the benefits of music education. MENC books, such as *Music Makes the Difference: Music, Brain Development, and Learning; Growing Up Complete: The Imperative for Music Education;* and . . . *And Music for All*, provide information on music and brain development, advocacy, and related topics. MENC staff members have compiled a list of music education facts and figures from a wealth of sources on the benefits conveyed by music education. These facts and figures are grouped into four categories: success in society, success in school, success in developing intelligence, and success in life (visit www.menc.org/information/advocate/facts.html). For a list of articles on academic achievement and music on the MENC website, visit www.menc.org/publication/articles/academic/academic.htm. The Arts Education Partnership promotes the role of the arts in the learning and development of every child and provides a wealth of resources on their website (www.aep-arts.org). NAMM has sponsored research showing that musical training affects brain development in young children. (Visit www.namm.org/press-room/press-releases and click on "Archive"; at the bottom of the page, click on "2006." Article is dated December 5, 2006.)

As these and other studies demonstrate, music education has important benefits. The resources cited here can serve to persuade administrators and local communities that these benefits are reason to build and support strong music education programs.

Advocacy Resources

Web Resources
- Advocacy Central on MENC's website: www.menc.org/information/advocacy/main.html.
- MENC position statement "Advocacy and the Music Educator," available online at www.menc.org/statements.
- MENC position statement "The Value and Quality of Arts Education," available online at www.menc.org/statements.
- NAMM-supported research on musical training and brain development on NAMM's website at www.namm.org. Visit press release archives for December 5, 2006.

Print Resources
- MENC. 2006. Sounding the theme: Advocacy programs work for us. *Teaching Music* 14(1):52–62.
- Orzolek, D. C. 2004. Electing music advocates. *Music Educators Journal* 91(2):13–17.
- MENC. 2004. MENC partners with arts groups to advocate music. *Music Educators Journal* 91(2):5.
- Burton, Suzanne L. 2004. Educate our advocates! *Music Educators Journal* 90(5):17–21.
- MENC. 2006. Principals say music programs affect graduation. *Teaching Music* 14(2):6.
- MENC. 2000. *Music makes the difference: Music, brain development, and learning.* Reston, Va.: Author.
- MENC. 1991. *Growing up complete: The imperative for music education.* Reston, Va.: Author.
- MENC. 2001. . . . *And music for all.* Reston, Va.: Author.

OBTAINING FUNDING OUTSIDE THE SCHOOL BUDGET

As stated in MENC's position statement on fund-raising, financial support for music education must be part of the school's or district's regular curricular budget. The position statement warns, "if not managed carefully, fund-raising activities may result in a loss of regular curricular budget funds and cause music to be classified as an 'extracurricular activity' and therefore not eligible for school budget support. . . . Fund-raising should not supplant or replace regular school or district funding." Fund-raising should be considered a way to enrich music instruction and to provide activities and materials that are not normally part of school or district budgets.

All selected Model Music Programs supplemented the school budget through other funding sources. The schools and districts sought out, applied for, and received funding from a variety of outside sources.

Wendy Bloom, the music teacher at Haley Elementary School (Fort Wayne, Indiana), applied for a $30,000 grant as part of the Technology Professional Development Program with the state of Indiana. Knowing that technology is expensive, Bloom used an opportunity for professional development in technology to acquire knowledge to bolster her application to the Indiana Department of Education. As a result, the school's music classroom is an Indiana Department of Education Technology-Enriched Model Classroom. The multiworkstation music technology lab with electronic keyboards, music software, digital instruments, MIDI, and multimedia tools provides students with an interactive curriculum aligned with computer-assisted instruction and piano lessons. By obtaining this grant, the teacher was able to equip her school with a lab that will provide many years of valuable instruction.

In addition, the Music Department of Haley Elementary obtained a $28,000 grant from the Indiana Department of Education in conjunction with a music technologies project focused on African music and culture. After being selected as an MENC Model Music Program, the school used the award to host Titos Sompa and the Mbongi Dance Theater for an interactive assembly on African music culture and received a National Education Foundation Grant to further extend the project.

Haley Elementary School's Music Department brought in almost $60,000 for its exclusive use. By seeking out sources of money and learning to put together a winning application, Haley serves as an example to both teachers and administrators of how to garner outside funds to improve music education equipment and to enhance learning programs.

Page Middle School is located in rural Arizona where 70 percent of its students qualify for free or reduced lunch. Fifty percent of the community is Native American. To augment its music education funds, the school obtained over $5,000 in At-Risk Student Grants. One At-Risk Student Grant provided

$2,800 for the Native Cultures Music Club; the other provided $2,300 for summer music camp scholarships.

Nora Davis Magnet School, a rural public elementary school, has taken advantage of funding provided by the Mississippi Whole Schools Initiative, a statewide arts education program, for seven years and has been a model school for the initiative for the past two years.

The East Meadow School District obtained a $10,000 grant from the Empire State Partnerships program to support its collaboration with the American Symphony Orchestra. This funding was recently increased to $25,000 and has supported a collaboration that benefits all students in the district, not just music students.

As these schools and districts demonstrate, music educators can find funds to augment school music budgets from many different sources. While grants and funding are no substitute for a good solid music program, they can be useful for purchasing needed equipment, whether for technology labs, instruments, or music stands. Such grants can also provide money for musical activities that can benefit the entire school, such as the African music and culture project at Haley Elementary. Government funds are available on both federal and state levels, and arts foundations and private industry often have funds available for educational programs as well. Some districts received funds from less traditional sources, such as the East Ramapo Central School District in Spring Valley, New York, which received an $8,000 grant for the marching band from its state senator's office. To assist educators with fund-raising, the article "Shaking the Money Tree: Fund-Raising and Grants" in the February 2001 issue of *Teaching Music* provides guidance on fund-raising and writing grants, as well as a list of resources. MENC's website also has information on fundraising, grants, and donations (www.menc.org/information/infoserv/Aid.html). Many states have information on available grants on their state department of education websites. When faced with reduced budgets for music education, resourceful administrators and teachers can find sources to cover expenses that are no longer funded.

Other schools have reached out to the community for funds to assist their music students. Page Middle School, a school with 685 students, reached out to the local electric workers union and received $300 for scholarships for music camp. Conners Emerson School (430 students) obtained a $770 grant from the local school union to develop a cross-curricular program called "Voices of the Underground Railroad." Nora Davis Magnet School (301 students) has successfully sought funds from local businesses and individuals to fund school activities, such as its opera and Cultural Arts Festival.

Parents and students have been an impressive source of funds for music programs. Two rural school districts are notable in their fund-raising efforts: the Kennard-Dale Music Boosters Association (part of the South Eastern School District in Pennsylvania, which has 3,281 students) raised $22,000 for choral gowns and ensemble outfits, and parents and students associated with Rutland City Public Schools (Vermont, 2,959 students) have raised $20,000 to $40,000 for a major annual trip and a trip to Florida every four years. Other money-raising activities include a Lip Sync Show (Conners Emerson School) to raise money for the strings program, T-shirt sales (Nora Davis Magnet School), and an annual concert put on by the district Music Department faculty (William Floyd School District, New York) to raise funds for music scholarships. Most of the PTOs of the selected music programs raise money for their schools' music programs and are a wonderful resource for music educators.

Funding Resources
- Financial Aid section of MENC's website: www.menc.org/information/ infoserv/Aid.html.
- MENC position statement "Fund-raising," available online at www.menc .org/statements.
- MENC. 2001. Shaking the money tree: Fund-raising and grants. *Teaching Music* 8(4):25–31.

COLLABORATION WITH PROFESSIONALS AND PROFESSIONAL ORGANIZATIONS

Half of the music programs selected either have active collaborations with a professional music organization or have commissioned compositions from noted or collegiate composers. Taking advantage of its proximity to New York City, the East Meadow School District has several collaborations with professional musicians. In a side-by-side program with members of the American Symphony Orchestra (ASO), funded by a grant, students rehearse and perform side by side with professional musicians. In addition, the ASO performs thematic concerts that link music to the visual arts, literature, politics, and history, and students attend the concerts and preconcert lectures in a cross-curricular learning experience. East Meadow previously had a string residency program with the New York Virtuosi Chamber Orchestra; has participated in programs sponsored by Carnegie Hall's Education Program, such as Global Encounters and LinkUP!; and has enabled students to take part in master classes with members of the New York Philharmonic and other noted artists. Also located close to New York City, the Nanuet Union Free School District has a middle school opera program that is connected to the Metropolitan Opera Guild.

While the rest of the country does not have the wealth of professional music organizations that are found in New York City, some organizations have national programs. For example the Metropolitan Opera Guild has the Creating Original Opera Program (COO), a week-long summer teacher training program that provides teachers with the necessary skills, information, and methodologies to guide their students through COO. Participating teachers develop an in-school opera with their students and incorporate the COO Program into their school curriculum. Over the past twenty years, more than 1,800 teachers in over 800 schools throughout the United States and around the world have participated. (For more information, visit www.metoperafamily.org/education/educators and click on "Creating Original Opera.")

Likewise, Carnegie Hall has the Carnegie Communities LinkUP! Program designed to strengthen relationships between orchestras and their local schools and communities. Operated by the Weill Music Institute, it assists regional orchestras and arts organizations in adapting Carnegie Hall's highly acclaimed LinkUP! Program in their own communities. (Visit www.carnegiehall.org. Click on "Explore and Learn," then "Schools and Teachers," then "Communities LinkUP!") At Nora Davis Magnet School (Mississippi), fourth- through sixth-grade classes were selected for participation in the Communities LinkUP! Program. The students worked with the Southern Mississippi Symphony Orchestra in a standards-based curriculum that culminated in an end-of-year performance with the orchestra. The program also provides professional development, curriculum support materials, and recorders.

Professional musicians in smaller communities have educational programs also. In Indiana, the Foundation for Art and Music in Elementary Education partners with the Fort Wayne Philharmonic for their Composition Project.

Approximately thirty-five select fourth-grade students collaborate with a composer on an original symphony, which is performed by the Fort Wayne Philharmonic.

Exposure to and collaboration with professional musicians can be of great benefit to music students. Such collaborations can give students a feel for the life of a professional musician and provide music mentors to inspire them in their own music making. While the collaborations of MENC's selected Model Music Programs have been with professional musicians in large city symphonies and such, the same benefits can be obtained with performing arts groups in smaller venues. The examples here have been with more traditional groups performing more classical repertoire, but local groups performing in other styles such as jazz, pop, rock, and world music offer opportunities as well.

Sometimes a composer can impact a music program. Conners Emerson School in rural Maine obtained funds from its PTSA to commission a composer from the University of Maine for its middle school orchestra. The William Floyd School District (New York) commissioned and premiered a composition by a Pulitzer Prize–winning composer, and Adlai E. Stevenson High School (Illinois) has commissioned several pieces with professional composers. These programs support composition curricula and motivate students.

In the September 2004 issue of *Music Educators Journal*, the article "Composers and Children: A Future Creative Force?" shares a composer's experience writing music for a middle school band and provides suggestions on funding and arranging a collaboration with a composer. A composer can create some first-rate music for young students and thereby add a new dimension to their music education. By commissioning a composer, a music director can capitalize on school resources (e.g., featuring a local harmonica player or setting a student's poems to music) or make the celebration of a school milestone truly special. Students enjoy participating in the decisions on a piece of music and feel special performing a premiere. For more information on benefits and how to commission a work, see "Commissioning New Works for Orchestra" in *Teaching Music*, April 1994. The American Composers Forum helps set up collaborations with composers, and its BandQuest Program has a series of music written especially for middle-level band by world-class composers. (Visit www.composers forum.org. Click on "Programs," then "Education.")

In its position statement "The Non-Educator Performer in the Music Classroom," MENC

> encourages professional collaborative relationships between music educators and visiting musicians and other presenters in the music classroom, with the understanding that these visiting musicians and presenters should make connections to the existing curriculum and work with educators to ensure student learning.

MENC also cautions that the "mere presence of a musician or presenter does not automatically guarantee education, or even enrichment, in a classroom." The position statement presents the music educator's role for working with performers and provides guidelines for before, during, and after an event that includes a visiting musician to ensure the program meets goals for student learning.

Professional Collaboration Resources

Web Resources

- MENC position statement "The Non-Educator Performer in the Music Classroom," available online at www.menc.org/statements.
- Metropolitan Opera Guild's Creating Original Opera Program: www .metoperafamily.org/education/educators. Click on "Creating Original Opera."
- Carnegie Hall's Communities LinkUP! Program: www.carnegiehall.org. Click on "Explore and Learn," then "Schools and Teachers," then "Communities LinkUP!"
- The American Composers Forum's BandQuest Program website: www.composersforum.org. Click on "Programs," then "Education."

Print Resources

- Colgrass, M. 2004. Composers and children: A future creative force? *Music Educators Journal* 91(1):19–23.
- MENC. 1994. Commissioning new works for orchestra. *Teaching Music* 1(5):38–39.

PARTNERSHIP WITH THE COMMUNITY

Most of the selected Model Music Programs have a symbiotic relationship with their communities. Educators need to show parents and the community at large the ways music helps their children develop and grow, and showcasing the goals and achievements of the music program and its participants helps drive this point home. Musical performances, adjudicated festivals, and other community events accomplish these goals and generate goodwill for the music program. In addition, they often result in financial and other support for the activities of the Music Department. It serves music educators well to hone their skills as communicators and diplomats to enlist the aid of the community in building a strong music program.

Model Music Program winners demonstrate different ways to connect with the larger community. Nora Davis Magnet School (Mississippi) discovered that once certain music programs got off the ground and demonstrated their value to the community, local businesses and individuals were willing to fund activities like the opera and the Cultural Arts Festival. In the Nanuet Union Free School District (New York), nothing happens without music. In addition to traditional performances, every orientation, tribute to retiring staff, and display of appreciation for the PTA has a musical element. As a result of this high visibility and the quality of Nanuet's music program, the *New York Times* credited the Music Department as one of the main reasons families move to the community. East Meadow (New York) also credits its high-quality music program as a reason families move to the district.

The William Floyd School District (New York) has a Community Out-Reach Program to bring live music to various venues throughout the community, and every year holds an All-District Elementary Festival featuring its band, chorus, and orchestra members. The Swallowtail Fiddlers of Conners Emerson School (Maine) perform at community events, such as benefit concerts, Chamber of Commerce events, homes for the elderly, and fundraisers. East Ramapo (New York) students perform for the community and senior citizens and at PTA meetings; they also participate in local and county festivals. Haley Elementary (Indiana) has six performing ensembles that each give between two and six concerts per year. Nora Davis (Mississippi) students perform for local festivals, clubs and service organizations, and the local hospital. At Nora Davis, the band, strings, and choir groups join with other art disciplines to present an Arts Explosion exhibit each year for the school and community. Through their performances, students have the dual opportunity to take pride in their accomplishments and their gift to the community. In turn, the community places a higher value on music in the schools because of its visibility.

A community that enjoys the performances of its music students frequently responds to the needs of the Music Department. In South Portland, Maine, the local playhouse is made available for talent shows of the Spurwink School. The city of Rutland, Vermont, has made a large investment in the arts, especially music. When the state made a funding change favorable to the city of Rutland, the community elected to use the funds to strengthen the arts. In addition, the school board has established a fine arts supervisor position for the district. As mentioned previously, schools have reached out to their communities for funds for scholarships for music camp (Page Middle School) and for an instructional grant to develop a unit on "Voices of the Underground Railroad" (Conners Emerson School). Communities want to invest in the next generation; performances allow the community to see the young people their tax dollars and donations support.

Several of the winning Model Music Programs made efforts to adapt their music programs to the realities and needs of the communities they serve. For example, because 75 percent of the students at Page Middle School (Arizona) are from remote areas, the music program has a Guitar Club. Rather than driving extremely long distances to orchestra or band rehearsals, students can make music at home on their guitars. In recognition of the Navajo culture represented in the school population, the school also has a Native Cultures Music Club. The Swallowtail Fiddlers group at Conners Emerson (Maine) grew out of the strong tradition of folk and Irish music in the community. The area has many small bands that play at local dances and pubs. Fiddlers fit in easily with these styles, and the group was formed with the hope that students could learn traditional music styles and apply them to real-life experience. As a result, students often fiddle with the school group and with their relatives.

Another way to reach out to the community is through the media. In addition to advertising music events in local newspapers, schools can arrange for broadcast of their music performances. Nanuet arranged for broadcast of its

"Song of the Year" from an eighth-grade songwriting class on the Cornell University radio station. By working with the media, educators can use musical events to raise awareness in their communities of the benefits school music brings to children. MENC provides members with resources for working effectively with local media to promote their music programs to their communities. In the August 2006 issue of *Teaching Music,* the article "Working with the Media" has suggestions for using the media as well as some Web resources.

Music in Our Schools Month (MIOSM), an MENC program observed in March each year, is an ideal way to advocate music education in the community. The purpose of MIOSM is to raise awareness of the importance of music education for all children and to remind communities that school is where all children should have access to music. MIOSM is an opportunity for music teachers to bring their music programs to the attention of the school and the community and to display the benefits of school music. One of the Model Music Program winners, the William Floyd School District (New York) actively participates in the MIOSM program with a series of in-school performances and community music events. For more information, visit www.menc.org/miosm.

In forging strong community ties, music educators need to demonstrate the levels of achievement sought and achieved by the music program and by individual students. By effectively winning community support, music educators can strengthen the music program and boost the self-esteem of its participants.

Resources for Partnering with the Community

- Music in Our Schools Month on the MENC website: www.menc.org/miosm.
- Mack, Michael L., ed. 1992. *The music educator and community music: The best of MEJ.* Reston, Va.: Author—a collection of articles on relating to community from *Music Educators Journal.*
- MENC. 2006. Working with the media. *Teaching Music* 14(1):58.

TECHNOLOGY

A wide variety of music technology is available, both hardware and software, and most of the selected music programs had some technology in their schools, both general technology and music technology. Most teachers are familiar with the music technology used in schools: music labs, MIDI keyboards, sound systems with recording capability, and software for accompaniment, sequencing, notation, recording, and editing.

What these tools can do above and beyond their obvious use is engender student enthusiasm for the music program. The South Eastern School District (Pennsylvania) reports that their music technology program has raised student interest and increased involvement in other areas of the music program. When its music lab first opened six years ago, it had one section of twenty-seven students. It currently has 10 sections and serves about 230 students. The courses Music Technology I, II, and III are open to all students in the school. Because these courses are hands on and creative in nature, students who cared little for music become more enthusiastic and expand their participation. An added bonus is that both special needs and gifted students have the opportunity to be musically and creatively successful at their own pace.

Music technology can also reach students not normally found in school music programs. Rutland City Public Schools (Vermont) uses its technical center program to attract a student population frequently overlooked in traditional music programs. The program attracts serious drum, keyboard, guitar, and bass players who can study jazz and contemporary music for one to two years. East Ramapo Central School District (New York) requires middle and high school students who do not participate in a performance ensemble to take the Keyboards/Computers course, giving students not in the traditional music programs the opportunity to participate.

While it can be easy to think that a program needs the latest technology available, often older equipment and software can be equally useful. When the South Eastern School District (Pennsylvania) upgraded its high school music technology lab, it installed the previous equipment in the middle school, where it is used for keyboard instruction, music theory, and instrument study units. They thus maximized their expenditure and expanded their technology program. Often music software requiring only a basic computer enables teachers and students to accomplish a host of tasks that simplify a teacher's life and engage students. Some software can be downloaded for free, such as Audacity, open source software for recording and editing sounds. (See "Audacity in Vocal Improvisation: Motivating Elementary School Students through Technology," *Teaching Music*, February 2007.) Other more modest forms of technology include tools as simple as recording devices like those used by the Spurwink School and Conners Emerson (both in Maine). Students never tire of hearing themselves on a recording. A camcorder can also be a useful tool in evaluating rehearsals and performances and for assessing students.

What do you do with technology once you have it? In 1994, MENC released the Opportunity-to-Learn Standards for Music Instruction as a guide to what schools should provide to help students achieve both the National Standards for Music Education in grades K–12 and the MENC prekindergarten music education standards. Because of the advances in music technology since then, MENC prepared an addendum to the opportunity-to-learn standards, the Opportunity-to-Learn Standards for Music Technology, to provide more specific guidance on taking advantage of new technologies to offer a curriculum in line with the National Standards. This document tells more specifically what equipment to buy and how to allocate those resources. For each level, specifications are listed for curriculum and scheduling, staffing and equipment, materials and software, and facilities. (To read the entire document, visit www.menc.org/publication/books/techstan.htm.) In addition, the MENC website has a technology section (www.menc.org/technology.html) that has several resources, including a technology bulletin board and a list of available e-books on technology. It also contains the article "How One Class with One Computer Composed Music," by Jack Siegel, from the April 2004 issue of *Teaching Music.*

MENC publications can assist music educators with technology decisions. The book *Spotlight on Technology in the Music Classroom* is a selection of articles from state music education association journals on various ways music educators can use technology. In addition, each issue of *Music Educators Journal* has reviews of software and books relating to technology in the "All Things Technology" Department designed to help music educators sift through the maze of available products and decide what programs can best benefit their students. In the February 2005 issue of *Teaching Music*, fifth-grade teacher Amy Casey shares her experience with managing technology in the classroom in the article "A Learning-Center Solution for Using Technology in Elementary Music."

The Model Music Programs have demonstrated that technology in the music program provides several important functions: It can provide a medium for students to demonstrate their musical creativity and expression. It breathes new enthusiasm into music study and can serve as a springboard into other areas of the music education program. It provides a means to address the various abilities of music education students, especially students with special needs. It can simplify the music teacher's preparation and evaluation tasks. From one classroom computer to a high-tech music lab, tapping the potential of music technology can enhance an already strong music program.

Technology Resources

Web Resources
- Technology section at the MENC website: www.menc.org/technology.html.
- MENC. 1999. *Opportunity-to-Learn Standards for Music Technology*. Reston, Va.: Author. Available at www.menc.org/technology.

Print Resources
- Casey, A. 2005. A learning-center solution for using technology in elementary music. *Teaching Music* 12(4):50–53.
- MENC. 2003. *Spotlight on technology in the music classroom*. Reston, Va.: Author.
- Sichivitsa, V. 2007. Audacity in vocal improvisation: Motivating elementary school students through technology. *Teaching Music* 14(4):49–51.
- Siegel, J. 2004. How one class with one computer composed music. *Teaching Music* 11(5):44–48.

SERVING STUDENTS WITH SPECIAL NEEDS

The two Model Music Programs selected in this category have special programs to serve the needs of students with special needs. The Spurwink School (Maine) is dedicated exclusively to these students, and William Floyd School District (New York), a district with a solid, well-rounded music program, has a districtwide Adaptive Arts Program. Winners in other categories find that their music technology program has served these students well (South Eastern School District and East Ramapo Central School District). As these programs demonstrate, students with disabilities can successfully participate in school music programs.

The Spurwink School serves fifty-five elementary and middle school students who were unsuccessful in public schools due to mental, behavioral, or developmental challenges. Its one music teacher works three days a week and has created a flexible program that he adapts to the needs and abilities of the students. The program is grounded in creativity and fostering positive musical experiences for the students, many of whom had never before taken a music class. The program includes performing within the limitations of confidentiality restrictions.

In the William Floyd School District's Adaptive Arts Program, a two-teacher team with dual certification in (1) art or music and (2) special education, music therapy, or art therapy works with students with disabilities in self-contained classes in a therapeutic and experiential program. Students have performance experiences in band and string instruments and in singing and movement. The adaptive team has an independent budget.

Both the South Eastern School District (Pennsylvania) and the East Ramapo Central School District (New York) have found that their music technology programs have enabled students with special needs to express their creativity musically. At East Ramapo, special education students use the keyboards and write and record their own music and perform for parents and teachers.

The Individuals with Disabilities Education Act (IDEA) is the guiding legislation for all educators working with students with special needs. The December 2006 issue of *Teaching Music* helps decipher this legislation for music educators and provides a list of resources in the article "The Basic IDEA: The Individuals with Disabilities Act in Your Classroom."

As the Spurwink School and William Floyd School District have shown, music programs can be adapted to meet the needs of students with disabilities with planning, collaboration, and flexibility. Schools or districts with smaller budgets can work to improve the resources and structures already in place in compliance with IDEA. MENC has a wealth of resources to assist educators in this endeavor. In its position statement "Inclusivity in Music Education," MENC describes the music educator's role and sets guidelines for achieving inclusivity. MENC publications share articles on serving students with special needs. The March 2006 issue of *Music Educators Journal* is dedicated to demonstrating ideas and programs for children with disabilities. The articles contain plans and techniques that have proven successful in several programs, as well as extensive lists of resources, recommendations, and strategies for music teachers. In the December 2005 issue of *Teaching Music*, a teacher of instrumental music shares his experience and recommendations in "Including Exceptional Students in Your Instrumental Music Program." The MENC website also has a Teaching Special Learners section (www.menc.org/publication/articles/ speciallearners.html) with the article "Teaching Special Learners: Ideas from Veteran Teachers in the Music Classroom" and tips and classroom management techniques. In his book *Reaching and Teaching All Instrumental Music Students*, music educator Kevin Mixon dedicates a chapter to effectively adapting teaching methods to elicit the best performance from students with special needs in inclusive classrooms. The MENC publication *Spotlight on Making Music with Special Learners* is a collection of articles by music educators on various aspects on this topic.

Resources for Working with Students with Special Needs

- Teaching Special Learners section of MENC website: www.menc.org/ publicaton/articles/speciallearners.html.
- MENC position statement "Inclusivity in music education," available online at www.menc.org/statements.
- Mixon, K. 2007. *Reaching and teaching all instrumental music students*. Lanham, Md.: Rowman & Littlefield Education.
- MENC. 2004. *Spotlight on making music with special learners*. Reston, Va.: Author.
- Walter, J. S. 2006. The basic IDEA: The Individuals with Disabilities Act in your classroom. *Teaching Music* 14(3):22–26.
- Schaberg, G., comp. 1988. *TIPS: Teaching music to special learners*. Reston, Va.: MENC.
- March 2006 Special focus issue on children with disabilities. *Music Educators Journal* 92(4).

MULTICULTURAL AND INTERDISCIPLINARY LEARNING

Music is an expression of culture. It's a natural link to people and a society's way of life. The Model Music Programs demonstrate a variety of ways to study culture and other disciplines through music. Some required grant money, but many used the resources at hand to create a multicultural, multidisciplinary learning experience.

The Haley Elementary School (Indiana) used grant money for a project focused on African music and culture using music technologies and later hosted an African dance company for an interactive assembly focused on African music and culture. This program not only exposed students to African music but also integrated other disciplines, such as social studies, history, and art.

The Nora Davis Magnet School (Mississippi) holds an annual Cultural Arts Festival that involves the entire school. Each year the school chooses a culture or country to be the focus of the festival, and the students and faculty collaborate to incorporate the culture into several disciplines (music, dance, history, geography) in preparation for the festival. On the day of the festival, the knowledge students have gained comes to life through performances by guest artists, hands-on activity stations, and a parade. With the entire school working together, the shared work and preparation make this a truly collaborative and interdisciplinary activity. With planning and collaboration, any school can model Nora Davis to enrich its education program.

In the same vein, Adlai E. Stevenson High School (Illinois) conducts a two-day, all-school fine arts festival every two years called Odyssey. The festival provides classes, seminars, and performances in visual arts, dance, drama, music, and media for all students and faculty. The classes and performances are presented by a variety of paid professional artists, and the program relies heavily on volunteers from the student population and the community. One interesting aspect is that students take classes alongside their teachers and witness that learning is a lifelong experience.

Several schools have looked to the makeup of their students for ideas to incorporate the culture of the community into the music program. Because Page Middle School (Arizona) has a student population that is 75 percent Navajo, sixth-grade general music students study world native cultures, including the Navajo culture, as well as those of China, Polynesia, North and South America, and Africa. Students study each culture's music, singing styles, and instruments and use Native American flutes, guitars, and world drums. They also have a Native Cultures Music Club. Conversely, because of the makeup of the Page community and its remote location, the introduction of European classical music is new and multicultural for these students.

Conners Emerson School (Maine) is located in a community with a strong British Isles heritage, and local instrumental groups supply music for country, square, and contra dances and pub music. As a result, the school has a multi-age Swallowtail Fiddlers group that plays jigs, reels, hornpipes, and ditties of America, Ireland, and Scotland. Members of the group not only perform as members of the Swallowtail Fiddlers but also often perform with their relatives and other members of the community.

To broaden their curriculum, music educators can look to their communities and ask "What is available in my community that would work in my music program?"

Several schools have chosen theme-based concerts to integrate music with other disciplines. At East Meadow School District (New York), students participate in thematic concerts and lectures given by the American Symphony Orchestra. In Nanuet (New York) the high school choral program studies music history, composer biographies, music theory, and artistic expression in preparation for theme-based concerts.

Other schools depend on a more localized collaboration between faculty members. At Nora Davis Magnet School (Mississippi), the music specialist and classroom teacher work cooperatively to teach both music and math concepts to kindergarten classes with "Mozart Math." In addition, classroom teachers at each grade level collaborate their planning efforts for a weekly music infusion day. After teachers select a skill, the music specialist figures out a way to present it musically while reinforcing a musical skill or meeting a National Standard.

Often a song can provide the springboard for cross-disciplinary study. At East Meadow School District (New York), a music composition about Rosa Parks served as a basis for study of the civil rights movement, and social studies classes attended a rehearsal of the high school band.

All of these ideas from the Model Music Programs serve as inspiration for what can be done in other schools and districts. Some of them require collaborations outside the school, but many rely on the creativity and ingenuity of a single school's student, teacher, and community population.

MENC has sought to serve its members by providing resources for multicultural and cross-disciplinary education, as well as a forum for debate on the pros and cons of such emphasis of study. Both *Music Educators Journal* and *Teaching Music* have printed several articles over the years, and MENC has published several books on this topic as well (see Multicultural and Interdisciplinary Learning Resources below).

Multicultural and Interdisciplinary Learning Resources

From Music Educators Journal
- India's music: Popular film songs in the classroom (September 2006)
- Eight simple rules for singing multicultural music (September 2006)
- Music that represents culture: Selecting music with integrity (September 2006)
- An instrumental approach to culture study in general music (May 2006)
- Opening the doors to diverse traditions of music making: Multicultural music education at the university level (May 2006)
- Using the Native American flute in a beginning instrumental classroom (January 2006)
- Colliding perspectives? Music curriculum as cultural studies (March 2005)
- Whose music? Music education and cultural issues (March 2005)
- Building your instrumental music program in an urban school (January 2005) (discusses nontraditional, multicultural ensembles)
- Interdisciplinary lessons in musical acoustics: The science-math-music connection (September 2004)

From Teaching Music
- Build a bridge from music to other disciplines: A successful cross-curricular project (April 2006)
- Teaching music beyond the notes: History, Whiteman, and *Rhapsody in Blue* (April 2005)

MENC Books:
- Reimer, B., ed. 2002. *World musics and music education: Facing the issues.* Reston, Va.: MENC.
- Campbell, P. S., ed. 1996. *Music in cultural context: Eight views on world music education.* Reston, Va.: MENC.

- Anderson, W. M., and P. S. Campbell. 1996. *Multicultural perspectives in music education.* Reston, Va.: MENC.
- Andrews, L. J., and P. E. Sink. 2002. *Integrating music and reading instruction: Teaching strategies for upper-elementary grades.* Reston, Va.: MENC.
- Hansen, D., E. Bernstorf, and G. M. Stuber. 2004. *The music and literacy connection.* Reston, Va.: MENC.

SCHEDULING AND OPPORTUNITY

Scheduling music classes involves several issues. In addition to providing time each week for students to learn music, schools normally establish requirements and guidelines to give all students the opportunity to receive a music education.

All of the selected music programs start music instruction in kindergarten or first grade, usually with one or two classes per week lasting thirty to forty-five minutes. Participation in band, orchestra, or chorus typically begins anywhere between grades 3 and 5, with grade 4 being the most common. Most ensembles that provide extra performance opportunities meet before or after school.

Many districts require music instruction. Both Conners Emerson (Maine) and Nanuet Union Free School District (New York) have a required violin class in second grade that has boosted participation in orchestras in later grades. Rutland City Public Schools (Vermont) has mandatory music instruction for grades K–9. At Page Middle School (Arizona), every sixth grader must take a music class. In East Ramapo Central School District (New York), every middle school student not in a performing group takes Keyboard/Computer class.

Many schools and districts, in following a philosophy that every student at every level should have access to instruction in music, open their classes and ensembles to all students (East Meadow, Page Middle School). In East Meadow School District (New York), high school students may take as many music classes as they can fit in their schedule. In the South Eastern School District (Pennsylvania), music technology classes satisfy a fine arts or a technology requirement and are open to all students. The high school has a one-credit fine arts requirement for graduation and offers a Survey of the Fine Arts class. In the Rutland City Public Schools (Vermont), middle schoolers have an "experiential" block for the first hour of every day when they can participate in orchestra, chorus, and concert band. At the high school level, every freshman in Rutland is required to take a half-credit fine arts survey course that is applied toward the one-credit fine arts requirement for graduation. William Floyd School District (New York) offers a Music in Our Lives course to fulfill the state arts requirement for graduation.

Opening the music program to all students with a desire to participate follows a long-held philosophy of MENC. Several of the Model Music Programs specifically stated their adherence to this philosophy. For example, when Conners Emerson (Maine) created the popular Swallowtail Fiddlers Club, the director opened it to any string student who wanted to participate. The East Ramapo Central School District (New York) is committed to providing every student with an opportunity to study music, and all students study music. The South Eastern School District (Pennsylvania) considers its greatest strength to be providing exciting, hands-on music instruction for all students, even at the high school level.

STANDARDS

The Model Music Programs possess a strategy for defining success, achieving it, and assessing progress. They follow national or state standards or sometimes both and align their mission statements with them. Many districts point out that they review the music curriculum periodically and revise or expand it as needed to maintain a standards-based curriculum.

MENC spearheaded the development of the National Standards for Arts Education and constructed the National Standards for Music Education. Various types of information relating to the standards can be found on the MENC website. Visit www.menc.org and click on "National Standards" in the left-hand column. In addition to the National Standards and other information on standards, strategies, and benchmarks for assessing programs, there is a link to state music education standards. See also the MENC books listed in the Standards Resources below.

Teaching according to the standards and assessing student progress improves music education; at the same time, it strengthens music's place as a core academic subject. When states and school districts adopt these standards, they are speaking out for quality in a part of education that has too often been treated as optional.

Standards Resources

- National Standards section of the MENC website: www.menc.org/standards.

MENC Books

- MENC. 1994. *National Standards for Arts Education: What every young American should know and be able to do in the arts.* Reston, Va.: Author.
- MENC. 1996. *Aiming for excellence: The impact of the standards movement on music education.* Reston, Va.: Author.
- MENC. 1996. *Performance standards for music: Strategies and benchmarks for assessing progress toward the National Standards, grades preK–12.* Reston, Va.: Author.
- Lindeman, C. A., ed. 2003. *Benchmarks in action: A guide to standards-based assessment in music.* Reston, Va.: MENC.
- Reimer, B., ed. 2000. *Performing with understanding: The challenge of the National Standards for Music Education.* Reston, Va.: MENC.
- MENC. 2005. *Spotlight on general music: Teaching toward the standards.* Reston, Va.: Author.

FACULTY

The Model Music Programs also show that hiring highly qualified teachers and providing them opportunities to develop professionally makes an enormous impact on the success of a music program. For example, the Music Department of the William Floyd School District (New York) has a philosophy to hire the best staff who are specialists in their area, and all music teachers in the district are certified in music. Teachers teach in their area of expertise, and the district fosters a culture of excellence. A full-time coordinator of music and chairperson oversee a department of forty-five teachers.

In addition to their credentials, dedication to their profession has been instrumental in creating excellent music programs. East Meadow (New York) describes its music staff as "an extremely dedicated group of individuals who are passionate about what they do." Jeff Shaw at the Spurwink School (Maine) has shown a dedication to building music programs through his work in summer camps, nursing homes, after-school programs, and correctional institutions for youth. Wendy Bloom at Haley Elementary is an active member of various local and state music education committees and local music education boards and is a mentor teacher for music education students from Indiana/Purdue University. These associations assist her as a professional and assist her school in building and maintaining an excellent music program. Some of the Model Music Programs specifically mention that their music faculties are active performers outside school, and Nanuet (New York) mentioned that their principals regularly appear as guest artists.

Once highly trained teachers are on staff, schools have various programs to help them begin their careers and to develop professionally. For example, William Floyd School District (New York) has a New Teacher Mentor Program that pairs new teachers with mentors in their disciplines. The program is designed to maximize the success of beginning teachers by acclimating them to the culture of their departments. At East Ramapo Central School District (New York), music teachers share ideas and work and plan together during monthly music staff development meetings.

Providing teachers the opportunity to collaborate with their peers facilitates professional development and broadens students' education. Some schools actively foster collaboration among curriculum teams on a regular basis. At Adlai E. Stevenson High School (Illinois), the administration fosters collaborative work and provides time for faculty teams to meet each week to collaborate. As reported in their submission, "much of what we have been able to achieve on behalf of our students has been the result of collaboration between band, choir, and orchestra faculty. Viewing ourselves as a single music faculty—rather than as independent divisions—is the theme of our working relationships." In addition, at Stevenson, team teaching is core to the performance ensemble instructional strategy. The school supports two certified teachers for each performance ensemble class. With this team-teaching approach, one teacher can conduct sectional rehearsals and help or assess individual students while the other conducts the ensemble rehearsal. The teacher partners share insights, collaborate on lesson planning, and share conducting responsibilities. In addition, each performance division maintains close ties with the junior high school faculty and programs to keep them abreast of the opportunities and expectations in high school. On the other side of the spectrum, the music faculty also has working relationships with area universities to help with the education of the next generation of teachers by serving as student teacher mentors and also to expose their students to college students preparing for careers in music.

Collaborations across disciplines, such as those in Nora Davis's Music Infusion Day and Cultural Arts Festival and Stevenson's Odyssey Program, help establish closer ties between regular faculty and music educators, who frequently feel professionally isolated. Such collaborations also increase the visibility of the music faculty in the school and in the greater community. As Janice Greisch at Page Middle School points out, "some of the best advocating can happen in department, team, or grade-level collaborative meetings." She believes that by supporting other school programs, participating in curricular changes for the school, and integrating other subjects and skills into the music classroom, music teachers can get the word out on the needs and benefits of the music program. She recommends music programs should "become so important to the whole education program at the school that they can't possibly do without you!"

CONCLUSION

The Model Music Programs selected represent a wide variety of excellent music programs across the country at all levels from rural to urban settings and at disparate funding levels. They reflect the wonderful, everyday work of school districts, administrators, and teachers who make a difference in the lives of their students. The lessons they share touch many areas involved in music education: how the support of administrators and the community can make a model program possible, how additional outside funding can enhance music programs, how collaboration with professional musicians can energize a music program, how partnering with the community can garner support for a music program, how technology can help a music program, how music can increase the participation of students with special needs, how music can help create a multicultural and multidisciplinary curriculum, how the adherence to standards can promote music as a core academic subject, and how a high-quality staff can be invaluable to the music program.

Thanks to the creativity and hard work of the educators behind the Model Music Programs, others can replicate some of the ideas, features, and methods presented to enhance their own music programs. Educators know the value of collaboration; it has been the core of MENC since its inception. How many

educators have left a conference session or in-service meeting eager to replicate what others have done? It is our hope that these Model Music Programs
will serve to both inspire and affirm the importance of the work of music educators everywhere. After reading about these excellent programs that reflect
the work of talented music educators, we hope that you are left thinking, "I
can do that in my school!"

7

Other Programs

In looking over submissions for the Model Music Program, we consistently found two essential elements: programs that were enthusiastically supported by districts and administrations that value the role of music education in the school and dedicated music teachers who go above and beyond their normal duties to provide their students with a quality program in line with local, state, and/or national standards. In addition, music directors were eager to provide all students access to music making regardless of their socioeconomic background or financial resources.

PROFESSIONAL DEVELOPMENT FOR MUSIC TEACHERS

Music teachers are the heart and soul of the music program, and they provide the blood, sweat, and tears. Several districts recognize that professional development and support for their teachers are essential to a high-quality music program. The program at the Atlanta Public Schools stood out. They not only ensure that all teachers participate in standard professional development courses, but in addition, the music staff is divided into ten clusters with an experienced lead music teacher for each. The lead music teacher provides support to the teachers in the cluster in the form of program planning, performance evaluation preparation, and instructional support. The district also provides a music scope and sequence for each level of instruction based on the Georgia Music Learning Connections as a framework for planning lessons. All new teachers are linked up with a mentor at their school and an additional music mentor. New music teachers receive orientation and support through monthly workshop sessions and discussion groups, and their performance is monitored by principals and other professional development staff.

Across the country, professional development for music educators is offered at the district, state, and national levels. One of the objectives of MENC: The National Association for Music Education is to support music educators and, in particular, new music educators. In the spring 2007 issue of the *Journal of Music Teacher Education,* the article "Importance of Various Professional Development Opportunities and Workshop Topics as Determined by In-Service Music Teachers" reports on a study to determine the types of professional development opportunities and workshop topics music educators find most useful. This article can serve as a guide to those designing professional development workshops, as well as to those deciding which workshops to attend. In addition, MENC books strive to provide music educators with the strategies, tips, and information to support them as they seek ways to improve their teaching. MENC's Strategies for Teaching series targets music teachers from prekindergarten through grade 12. Each publication focuses on a specific curricular area and a particular level and includes teaching strategies based on the content and achievement standards. The TIPS series covers topics from classroom management to special learners and from establishing a string and orchestra program to music activities in early childhood. The Spotlight series are collections of articles from state music education association journals on topics ranging from early childhood music education to teaching band, chorus, or orchestra and from assessment to technology. *Spotlight on Transition to Teaching Music* focuses on recruitment and retention of music teachers, discussing issues such as mentoring, teacher shortages, burnout, and professional development options.

In addition, MENC maintains online resources for band, chorus, general music, orchestra, and technology. For each discipline, there is an online bulletin board, teachers' guides and lessons, and an "Information Please!" link to a variety of music education topics of interest to teachers, parents, students, and researchers. The online bulletin board for each discipline features expert mentors who rotate on a monthly basis and respond to questions every few days. Others in the profession respond as well, so mentors identify themselves as such. While only MENC members can post questions, anyone can read through the questions and responses.

Zoltán Kodály inspired music teachers to provide the best of all possible learning experiences and to seek out ways to better themselves as musicians and teachers. He reflected,

> It is much more important who is the music teacher in Kisvárda than who is the director of the opera house in Budapest . . . for a poor director fails once, but a poor teacher keeps on failing for thirty years, killing the love of music in thirty batches of children. (quoted in Choksy, 1974, p. 7)

Professional Development and Support Resources

Print Resources

- MENC's Spotlight series, Strategies for Teaching series, and TIPS Series: visit MENC's copublisher, Rowman & Littlefield Education, online at www.rowmaneducation.com. Under "Co-Publishers," click on "MENC," then on "S." The Spotlight series and Strategies for Teaching series are on pages 1–3. To see what is available in the TIPS series, click on "MENC" under "Co-Publishers," then on "T." The TIPS series is on the second page.
- Boardman, Eunice. 2002. *Dimensions of musical learning and teaching: A different kind of classroom.* Reston, Va.: MENC.
- Bush, Jeffrey. 2007. Importance of various professional development opportunities and workshop topics as determined by in-service music teachers. *Journal of Music Teacher Education* 16(2):10–18.
- Conway, Colleen M. 2003. *Great beginnings for music teachers: Mentoring and supporting new teachers.* Reston, Va.: MENC.
- Hansen, Dee. 2002. *Handbook for music supervision.* Reston, Va.: MENC.
- Kitchen, Bob. 2003. *It's your first year teaching, but you don't have to act like it.* Reston, Va.: MENC.
- MENC. 2004. *Teacher to teacher: A music educator's survival guide.* Reston, Va.: Author.
- Moore, Marvelene C. 2002. *Classroom management in general, choral, and instrumental music programs.* Reston, Va.: MENC.

Web Resources

- MENC Bulletin Boards: visit www.menc.org, in the left-hand column, click on the appropriate discipline (band, chorus, general music, orchestra, or technology) and scroll down to the link for the bulletin board. Other resources for each discipline are also available.
- MENC Ask the Mentors: visit www.menc.org/mentors to see the featured mentors for each discipline by month and to read their biographical information.

MUSIC FOR ALL

Another recurring theme in the program submissions was the desire to make music education available to all students regardless of socioeconomic circumstances. Most programs make instruments available to their students at no cost. One school reported that only 2 out of 150 students own their own instrument. One music director told us about building up an inventory of a dozen used band instruments over time so that low-income students can borrow one and participate in the program. One district reported that all students in the instrumental program who desire private instruction receive lessons from professional instructors paid from the district music budget. Another district reported that over half of its student population participates in the Title I free- or reduced-lunch program, and 100 percent of its students participate in the music program every year. Frequently, the general music program in elementary school is required of all students; however, music directors and administrators have demonstrated their desire to have the participation of students at all levels who wish to do so by offering the opportunity and the equipment to make it happen.

MENC addresses the issue of music for all in its position statement "Inclusivity in Music Education." MENC emphasizes that "excluding some Americans from music education denies them access to one of the core academic subjects, music, as an essential path toward meeting their educational needs, breaking social and economic barriers, and accommodating diverse learning and teaching. Music education must involve and serve individuals from all demographic strata in our society." The position statement defines the music educator's role in this issue as follows: "(1) to strive to ensure that all students have access to music programs that address achievement in all nine areas set forth in the National Standards, (2) to present a curriculum that encompasses a wide variety of styles and genres of music, and (3) to embrace the best instructional techniques and practices."

Resources for Music for All
- MENC position statement "Inclusivity in Music Education," available at www.menc.org/connect/surveys/position/inclusivitystatement.html.
- MENC. 2001. . . . *And music for all.* Reston, Va.: Author.
- MENC. 1991. *Growing up complete: The imperative for music education.* Reston, Va.: Author.
- MENC. 2000. *Music makes the difference: Music, brain development, and learning.* Reston, Va: Author.

VISIBILITY IN THE COMMUNITY
Lucky music directors operate in communities that are already excited about music or have worked hard to get their communities on board. Such communities donate time, talents, and money in support of music programs. In addition to their teaching duties, music teachers have the added responsibility of displaying the talents and efforts of their students. Visibility through performance also helps a music program grow by attracting new participants.

The Model Music Program submissions had ideas for music performance and sharing the music program with the larger community. In addition to traditional concerts and competitions, there were other performance ideas that occurred outside the school community:

- Several elementary school bands joined together to perform in one location for evening concerts that reached a broader audience than a single-school event would.
- A third-grade recorder ensemble performed at a school board meeting to a standing-room-only crowd.
- Students performed at several community events, such as Veterans Day and at tree-lighting ceremonies.
- Students performed at senior centers and convalescent hospitals.

One music director commented, "the high school groups perform in the community regularly, and the community has come to expect great things." For more ideas on partnering with your community, see chapter 7. The MENC publication *TIPS: Public Relations* is full of suggestions on a variety of public relation topics and has a bibliography.

SPECIAL PROGRAMS

The Model Music Program submissions showed us that music directors use a variety of programs to spark student interest and increase participation in the music program. In addition to traditional ensembles, music directors have instituted many innovative groups that offer a variety of musical and cultural styles:

- Urban Youth Harp Ensemble—a blend of thirty middle and high school students who take lessons twice a week from the principal harpist of the Atlanta Symphony Orchestra. Because it's uncommon, the harp can generate surprise and excitement. For information relating to the harp, see *Harp Column* magazine, which is published six times a year and has a website with several online forums, including ones for teaching harp and harp students, as well as information on the Young Artists Harp Seminar. The American Harp Society has a list of published harp parts for school ensembles for grades 1–12 (www.harpsociety.org, click on "Resources," then on "Education Project 2000" under "Education" in the left-hand column) and maintains a list of harp teachers organized by state. The article "Pulling Strings to Get a Harp in Your School" in the April 1984 issue of *Music Educators Journal* discusses attracting harp students and obtaining harps. In addition, the May 2007 issue of MENC's Mariachi Newsletter contains the article "Teaching the Mariachi Harp" (www.menc.org, click on "Mariachi" in the left-hand column, then click on "Newsletter Archive").
- Secondary Mariachi Program—a program that has brought in numerous students to music programs, students who did not participate in music ensembles previously. Because of a lack of repertoire for sale, one director has students write their own arrangements of traditional melodies. As students learn the role of their instruments, this task becomes easier. MENC has a host of Mariachi resources on its website, including a forum, newsletter, methods and sheet music, curriculum, and resources. Go to www.menc.org and click on "Mariachi" in the left-hand column. See also the article "Mariachi: Ethnic Music as a Teaching Tool" in the February 2002 issue of *Teach-*

ing Music, which covers all aspects of Mariachi, including a section on getting started and resources.

- Steel Drum Program—a program used in both elementary and secondary schools that often features music from other cultures. See the new MENC book, *The Steel Band Game Plan: Strategies for Starting, Building, and Maintaining Your Pan Program* by Chris Tanner. In addition to providing a comprehensive how-to for starting a pan program, the author provides resources of suggested readings, recordings, sources of sheet music, and conferences and workshops. See also "African Drum and Steel Pan Ensembles" in the August 2000 issue of *Teaching Music.*

- School of Rock—a combination of performance, composition, and theory. It has drawn students who otherwise might not participate in the music program and who learn music theory and perform some of their original compositions. See the article "Bach and Rock in the Music Classroom" in the December 2000 issue of *Teaching Music* for a compilation of ideas on this issue from several music educators. The Rock and Roll Hall of Fame website has several resources for teachers at www.rockhall.com/teacher.

- Garage Band 101—an after-school program that focuses on contemporary instruments and music where students perform in their own bands. One director reported that teaching kids through music they can relate to causes them to blossom as musicians and as people. The MENC book *Bridging the Gap: Popular Music and Music Education,* edited by Carlos X. Rodriguez, is a collection of essays by well-known scholars and educators addressing important topics, such as the many possible definitions of popular music, information on how popular musicians learn, and specific examples of educational programs that incorporate popular music.

- Drumming Class—a class found to boost motivation and blend music study with lessons in multiculturalism and diversity, as well as fostering team building, respect, listening, and problem solving. See the *Teaching Music* articles "Drumming: The Future Is in Your Hands" (December 2001) and "African Drum and Steel Pan Ensembles" (August 2000) for more on the benefits and how-tos of drumming.

- Bow-Dacious String Band—a group devoted to learning excellent ensemble skills, improvisation, and applied music theory through performance of a variety of popular music genres with an emphasis on group effort. For information and how-to, see the MENC publication *TIPS: Establishing a*

String and Orchestra Program and the article "How We Started a Fiddle Group" in the December 2000 issue of *Teaching Music.*

- Summer Marching Band Program—a program that helps inexperienced freshmen prepare for the fall season by meeting for two weeks before the school year begins. The program also creates cohesion and a sense of esprit de corps. The dedicated director runs the program without funding.

- Jazz, Show, or Swing Choir—unlike a traditional choir or Glee Club, a jazz, show, or swing choir performs contemporary music with choreography and is often accompanied by piano, bass, and drums. Broadway show tunes, pop music hits, old standards, and secular holiday music make up the typical swing choir repertoire. Frequently students create choreography routines for the group. The MENC book *Getting Started with Jazz/Show Choir* discusses various aspects from recruitment to outfits and has a chapter on choreography. For information on incorporating dance with music, see "Dance in the Music Classroom" in the August 1998 issue of *Teaching Music,* which discusses teaching dance design, mentions specific dance steps, and points out cross-curricular connections. "Dance in the Music Curriculum" in the May 1996 issue of *Music Educators Journal* emphasizes multicultural aspects of combining dance with music instruction, as well as various dimensions relating to dance, such as purpose, location, use of imagery and props, movement style, and musical accompaniment.

- Musical Drama Program—an elementary school music program that emphasizes songwriting and has an after-school program where thirty students write their own musical drama with song and dance. Students write songs about meaningful feelings, as well as important science, math, and social studies figures and events for an interdisciplinary experience. Student songs are recorded on cassette to take home or performed in front of their classmates; some songs are selected for schoolwide concerts and assemblies. While the program emphasizes National Standard 4, composing and arranging music within specified guidelines, all other standards are integrated with the songwriting emphasis, including writing, reading, singing, analyzing, and relating music to history and culture. All students are encouraged to express their ideas in music and to perform their work in public. Lead performance roles (solos) are given only to students who audition and meet moderate musicianship standards and who meet their classroom teacher's learning expectations (usually a grade of B or higher in core subjects). All students are encouraged to meet these standards, and many students significantly improve their grades so they can participate. For more information on guiding students in composing, see "5 Steps for Leading Students in Classroom Composing" in the April 2007 issue of *Teaching Music*. For suggestions on helping students compose, see "Making Composition Work in Your Music Program" in the September 2003 issue of *Music Educators Journal*. The April 2003 issue of *Teaching Music* has several articles on composition and improvisation in observance of Jazz Appreciation Month: "Take a Chance with Aleatory Composition," which has several lesson plans and ideas; "Step by Step: Using Kodály to Build Vocal Improvisation"; "Beginning Steps to Improvisation"; and "Phone-ominal Composition: A Startup Approach," which begins students composing using their own phone numbers and assigning a letter on the C scale to the numbers 1–9. See also the MENC books *Composition in the Classroom: A Tool for Teaching* by Jackie Wiggins and *Why and How to Teach Music Composition: A New Horizon for Music Education*, edited by Maud Hickey.

- Guitar Program—an opportunity to study the single most popular instrument among young people. Experience has shown that this group attracts new students rather than siphoning them off from band or choir. The MENC website has a guide to guitar in the classroom, with information on setting up a guitar class, curriculum guidelines, a lesson plan for improvising, a history of guitar from its origins in Persia to the post-MIDI virtual guitar, and a list of resources. Visit www.menc.org/music_classes/guitar/intro.html and click on "Begin Guide" in the lower right-hand column. The MENC publication *Strategies for Teaching Middle-Level and High School Guitar* contains lesson plans based on the National Standards and a list of resources.
- Gospel Choir—a group that may serve the needs of underrepresented students and allow participants to experience another culture. Gospel choirs also give participants an opportunity to think about race and racial bias and to strengthen their aural and improvisational skills. In its position statement "Sacred Music in Schools," MENC states, "the study and performance of religious music within an educational context is a vital and appropriate part of a comprehensive music education. The omission of sacred music from the school curriculum would result in an incomplete educational experience." However, MENC cautions, "with this volatile topic, music educators

should exercise caution and good judgment in selecting sacred music for study and programming for public performances." To read MENC's position statement, visit www.menc.org/statements. For more information on gospel choirs, see the article "Developing a Gospel Choir" in the January 2003 issue of *Music Educators Journal.*

- Marimba Ensemble—while marimba music originated in Africa, it spread to the Caribbean, Latin America, and beyond and appeals to students of many different backgrounds. For information on music for the marimba, read "The Total Spectrum of Marimba Repertoire" by Gifford Howarth, a professor focusing on marimba techniques at Penn State University, on the Web at www.yamaha.com/yamahavgn/Documents/BandOrchestra/Percussion _Tips_Howarth.pdf

- Basketball Pep Band—normally a group of students who are also part of a larger ensemble like a marching band or concert band. Pep bands usually perform at pep rallies or sporting events. The MENC publication *Spotlight on Teaching Band*, comprised of selected articles from state music education association journals on the topic of band, covers all aspects of teaching band. In the Marching and Pep Bands section, the article "Stump the 'Jock'"addresses the role of the band in activity programs as viewed by coaches, administrators, and band directors. Some schools establish a basketball pep band to alleviate the burden of band members playing at all ball games.

- Recorder Ensemble—an excellent medium to explore musical concepts and to develop music appreciation. It also supports understanding music in relation to history and culture, National Standard 9. To find out how to set up a recorder ensemble, read "Introducing Recorder Ensembles in General Music Class" from the Spring 2000 issue of *General Music Today*, available from member services of MENC (mbrserv@menc.org or 800-828-0229). The book *Playing the Soprano Recorder* by Lois V. Guderian is also available from MENC and teaches music reading and creative thinking.

- Madrigal Ensemble—an a capella group of four to six voice parts of a secular text dating back to thirteenth and fourteenth century Italy. Singers enjoy dressing in period costumes. Madrigal ensembles also connect to understanding music in relation to history and culture, National Standard 9. The article "Revisiting the Madrigal Ensemble" in the October 1995 issue of *Teaching Music* discusses organizing a madrigal ensemble, choosing literature, and meeting National Standard 1. For madrigal repertoire, see *The Oxford Book of English Madrigals*, edited by Philip Ledger (Oxford: Oxford University Press, 1979) and *The Oxford Book of Italian Madrigals*, edited by Alec Harmon (Oxford: Oxford University Press, 1983).

- Handbell Program—a group that has drawn interest from students who otherwise would not be interested in music in addition to those who are. For information on starting a handbell program, see *Handbell Helper: A Guide for Beginning Directors and Choirs* by Martha Lynn Thompson (Nashville, Tenn.: Abingdon Press, 1996) and *Meeting the National Standards with Handbells and Handchimes* by Michael B. McBride and Baldwin Marva (Lanham, Md.: Scarecrow Press, 1999). The American Guild of English Handbell Ringers has a website (www.agehr.org), learning events, and a bimonthly journal called *Overtones.*

All of the above programs attest to the creativity and dedication of music educators, as well as the variety of traditional and nontraditional musical experiences available to capture students' interest.

Other submissions spoke of various programs to enhance more traditional programs. Some of these programs involve the use of visiting musicians and other presenters. MENC has issued a position statement, "The Non-Educator Performer in the Music Classroom," that encourages professional collaborative relationships between music educators and visiting musicians and other presenters. However, MENC recommends, "these visiting musicians and presenters should make connections to the existing curriculum and work with educators to ensure student learning." Partnerships with arts and cultural organizations can be important resources for schools and can positively affect student learning, but noneducator performers must work with the highly qualified teacher who is in charge of music instruction. The position statement sets forth the role of the music educator and guidelines for working with individuals or organizations from the music profession.

Ideas for enhancing music programs from our submissions follow:

- Create a Symphony—an education program of the New York Pops in which a professional composer takes up residence in a select New York City public school. The program fosters a means for students to understand and express basic musical concepts by creating a musical narrative of their thoughts, ideas, and feelings. The program gives nonmusic students, particularly in high-risk schools, the opportunity to experience the freedom, joy, and limitless possibilities in the creative process and to open new channels and outlets for their prolific energy, both positive and negative. Students learn to express themselves freely, without judgment. The program has proven to be a very positive experience that has translated to every aspect of the participants' lives. The program is structured so that students are always successful and cannot fail. For more information on this and other education programs of the New York Pops, visit www.newyorkpops.org/html/education.html.

- Artist-in-Residence—an annual program where a visiting artist is in residence at school for two weeks. In the school submitting this idea, all students work directly with the artist, and forty select students work with him or her daily for a more in-depth experience. For guidance on using an artist-in-residence program, read "Bringing Artists into the Classroom" in the September 1992 issue of *Music Educators Journal*. Many residency programs are supported by the Arts in Education Program of the National Endowment for the Arts (www.nea.gov), and state arts agencies often support artist residency programs as well, such as the North Dakota Council on the Arts, the Virginia Commission for the Arts, and the California Arts Council.

- Broadway Musical—a musical with songs, choreography, and dramatic roles. This can be a collaborative effort with each class performing a song and dance on stage, while other classes act as the backup group. Each class can create its own props, working with both the music and classroom teachers. If there is a theater in your area performing a musical, students could benefit from attending the productions. One New York school takes its Broadway choral group to Broadway to see performances and participate in workshops with cast members. For music educators who are off-off-Broadway, local theater and touring groups can be just as enriching. The ASCAP Foundation has a Children Will Listen Program that offers students the opportunity to experience musical theater (www.ascapfoundation.org, click on "Community Outreach"). Broadway Across America offers several programs in its Education Department: local programs across the country offer educational programs to foster a better understanding and appreciation of theater via touring productions; official study guides with show-specific overviews of plots, characters, themes, and historical and cultural significance; and features on various aspects of the theater, such as understudies and touring productions, called Broadway 101 (visit www.broadwayacross america.com and click on "Education").

- Year-End Sing—groups of fifteen to twenty fourth- and fifth-grade students perform with the faculty band to lead the whole school in singing. Besides being an enjoyable event, students learn that music is a lifelong pursuit.
- Salute to Music—another education program of the New York Pops in which New York Pops instructors provide free lessons to students in each of New York City's five boroughs. The lessons are offered as part of the New York Department of Education's boroughwide Band and Orchestra Program, a voluntary after-school program for students who wish to study music but whose schools have limited resources. Professional instructors provide lessons in all the major instrument groups, including strings, woodwinds, brass, and percussion. At the end of the year, more than two dozen select Salute to Music students perform on the Carnegie Hall stage with the New York Pops at the orchestra's gala concert. The program provides a unique, multicultural, diverse cross-section of students who come together to play music with the same joyful goal. For more information about the program, visit www.newyorkpops.org/html/ed-salute_to_music.html. For those outside the New York City area, most cities and towns have performing musical groups nearby who either have established education programs or who are willing to work with local schools to enhance their music programs. See chapter 6, "Collaboration with Professionals and Professional Organizations" for other possibilities for collaborating with professional groups.
- Arrowhead Area Consortium Band—a collaboration that provides small districts with a large-group ensemble experience three or four times a year. Normally, students have an opportunity for this type of experience only once a year. Each participating school has a local program with a band director onsite and presents concerts on its own but at the same time supports the consortium. The students who stay with the program through eighth grade go on to high school knowing the members in the consortium band, making the transition to high school a little easier. This five-school cooperative shares a budget and works together as a team.

RESOURCE FOR SPECIALIZED ENSEMBLES

- Cutietta, Robert A., ed. 1999. *Strategies for teaching specialized ensembles.* Reston, Va.: MENC. This compilation correlates the National Standards for Music Education with lesson plans for various ensembles ranging from madrigal singers to handbell choirs and from rock bands to Cuban percussion ensembles.

INTERDISCIPLINARY AND MULTICULTURAL CONNECTIONS

In addition to the value of music study for its own sake, music frequently provides links to interdisciplinary and multicultural topics. Some districts base the music curriculum on character education themes and integrate character education into every lesson. One school has a team-building choral program to teach students to work together cooperatively in the pursuit of a common goal. In that vein, a music director at a school located in an area with one of the highest crime rates in Oakland commented, "during music, our students learn songs about respect, diversity, conflict resolution, and getting along with others. Our program is not just about music; it is about inspiring our students to become all that they can." While funding cuts killed this successful program in other Oakland schools, this school retained the program with the support of the principal, choosing to cut other programs instead.

Many submissions mentioned integrating other core disciplines with the arts. One music director mentioned that core subject material is blended with the music taught to help students memorize material with song. Another commented that music "can assist in teaching students the basics of math, English, and history in a most enjoyable and fun way." One school is in the process of "enhancing core subjects through music" both in the music and regular classrooms based on research showing that music can scaffold student success and promote academic achievement. Another school received the Hewlett Packard Technology for Teaching Grant that included a music specialist to integrate music into the first- and second-grade science and math curricula. For resources on multicultural and interdisciplinary learning, see chapter 6.

STUDENTS WITH SPECIAL NEEDS

Frequently music instruction captures students' interest and emotions unlike any other subject. It also feeds the human need for creativity and self-expression. While the topic of working with students with special needs is addressed in chapter 6, one teacher pointed out poignantly just how much music can mean to these children:

> Many of my students come from disadvantaged homes or foster care. I also have students who are at group homes and ones who live independently. I also teach many special education students and have taught visually disabled and mentally disabled students. All of these students have gained some kind of confidence in themselves through this music program. I have also been told that the only reason most of these students come to school is solely for the purpose of singing in my program.

Another submission described the Fingersteps Music Program, a program developed by a father for his two children with cerebral palsy to allow them to participate in family music sessions. The program enables students with special needs to participate fully in music with a goal toward streamlining into traditional band programs. The program uses wireless MIDI devices that enable children with physical disabilities to compose and perform music. The students perform as an ensemble similar to a handbell choir, playing together as a single musician. The MIDI devices can be configured to play single notes, chords, MIDI, or other sound files, as well as to assist students with improvisation. The designer has identified software and hardware requirements to enable students with a variety of abilities to perform together in a single ensemble and is developing a library of ensemble pieces to help students master their adaptive musical instruments and improve their skills. For more information about this program, visit www.fingersteps.org.

FINANCIAL SUPPORT FOR MUSIC PROGRAMS
The arts were designated a core academic subject when the No Child Left Behind Act was reauthorized. As a core subject, financial support for music education must be part of the school's and district's regular curricular budget. When budgeted funds fall short, music educators turn to fund-raising to maintain the quality program the community expects. However, if not managed carefully, fund-raising activities may result in a loss of regular curricular budget funds. (Make sure that any publicity about fund-raising activity refers to it as *supplemental* to the regular budget.) Nevertheless, raising additional

funds outside the budget is often a part of life for music teachers. In addition to purchasing musical instruments and equipping music labs, there are repair and maintenance costs that may fall outside scheduled maintenance. Performing ensembles need uniforms and money to cover the costs of trips to perform and compete within and without their school districts. As mentioned in more detail in chapter 6, the model programs have demonstrated ways to supplement funds included in the music program budget, if there is one. The other program submissions also demonstrate various ways to raise money.

One of the recurring methods for fund-raising is through a booster club. Many programs have booster clubs specific to a particular ensemble, such as a Choral Parents Booster Club or the Band Booster Club. Other schools may pool their efforts in one booster organization called a Music Booster Club that supports all the ensembles. Frequently, booster organizations are comprised of parents, but many also include members of the community with an interest in music. An independently operated booster organization can take on the main fund-raising efforts and free music directors to focus exclusively on the music program. One advantage of including community members and organizations in the booster club is to provide some permanence in membership because parents move on as their children graduate. In some areas where school policy prohibits the music program from doing any fund-raising, an independent booster club can take over those responsibilities. Booster organizations raise money for various purposes: uniforms, equipment, trips, scholarships, and so forth.

Before establishing a booster club, music educators should read MENC's position statement on fund-raising (www.menc.org/statements). Any booster group should be officially recognized and endorsed by the school's administration. In addition, booster organizations should be incorporated under your state's not-for-profit laws. Among the roles a music educator plays as a manager of the booster club, he or she should be knowledgeable about the local board of education and school policies regarding fund-raising, as well as the fiscal and political ramifications. Because schools and districts have different requirements and policies governing how money raised by booster organizations is to be handled, accounted for, and deposited, the music educator should know this information up front. For more information on organizing, budgeting, fund-raising, publicity, travel, and achieving school and community support, see the MENC book *Music Booster Manual*.

Students are frequently involved in fund-raising for the music program, although some schools prohibit their participation. Popular fund-raising activities include product sales, car washes, raffles, auctions, ad sales, and door-to-door requests or special fundraiser performances. Before beginning a fundraising project, administrators, teachers, and parents should ensure that the planned activity is appropriate for students and adheres to the Code of Ethics endorsed by MENC and its partners (see www.menc.org/publication/books/ethics.html). Some schools take the profits of such fundraisers and give them back to the students based on their personal sales in the form of student savings accounts to offset payments on uniforms, trips, band camp, or other music activities. Sometimes the school's Tri-M Honor Society demonstrates leadership in fund-raising activities.

Many music programs supplement their funds with grants. There is a wide variety of sources for grant monies. For communities of lower economic means, grant writing is an especially attractive alternative to reaching out to families who are already stretched financially; however, because of budget cutbacks, grant writing is also common in some of the wealthiest school districts. A sampling of grant sources mentioned in the submissions follows:

Private

- United Way—a network of over 1,200 United Ways across the country work with local communities on various community issues, including helping children succeed (www.unitedway.org).
- Bright Ideas Grants offered by power companies—a classroom enrichment grant program designed to reward creative and innovative ideas in classroom instruction that will enhance the learning experience for students. Visit your local power company's website to see if they participate or have their own educational grant program.
- Mr. Holland's Opus Foundation—supports music education through the donation of new and refurbished musical instruments to underserved school and community music programs and individual students nationwide (www.mhopus.org).
- Best Buy Te@ch Awards—rewards schools using interactive technology to make learning fun (communications.bestbuy.com/communityrelations/teach.asp).

- Lied Foundation—a private foundation giving grants and scholarships in the field of education (3907 West Charleston Boulevard, Las Vegas, Nevada 89102, 702-878-1559).
- VH1 Save the Music Foundation—dedicated to restoring instrumental music education in the United States and raising awareness of the importance of music education as part of a child's education. The foundation purchases new musical instruments to restore music education programs that have been cut due to budget reductions in the past or to save programs at risk of elimination due to lack of instruments. The foundation also conducts awareness campaigns, musical instrument drives, and fund-raising events (www.vh1.com/partners/save_the_music).
- Mattel Children's Foundation—makes grants to 502(c)3 nonprofit organizations (such as a booster club) that benefit children in need (www.mattel .com/about_us/philanthropy, click on "Programs," then click on "Grant-making").
- Hewlett Packard Technology for Teaching—supports innovative and effective uses of technology in the classroom setting, granting awards to K–12 public schools that are using a collaborative, team-based approach, especially in communities where HP has a presence (www.hp.com/hpinfo/ grants/us/programs/tech_teaching/index.html).

Local
- Large companies often have education programs for schools located near company facilities. For example, the GlaxoSmithKline Education Program supports educational programs in Research Triangle Park, North Carolina, and Philadelphia, Pennsylvania (us.gsk.com/html/community/community -education-programs.html). The Disneyland Resort Enabling Grants Program was created for local school districts in and around the Anaheim area. The program provides classroom teachers with needed funds for projects, programs, and materials that directly support the involvement of students in the visual and performing arts (publicaffairs.disneyland.com/education, click on "Enabling Grants" in the left-hand column). If a large company resides near your school district, explore its website for educational programs.
- Municipalities frequently have educational programs that offer financial support. Some of the local groups granting funds mentioned in the submissions include the following:

- Nashville Alliance for Public Education
- Charles Gray Award from the Pittsburgh Civic Light Opera
- City Heights (San Diego) Educational Pilot/Price Charities Foundation
- Hermiston (Oregon) Education Foundation
- Meyer Memorial Trust (Oregon and Washington)
- City of Whittier, California, Cultural Arts Foundation

Government

- Title I—a federal program that provides funds to state departments of education, local school districts, and schools to provide quality opportunities for students in low-income schools (www.ed.gov/programs/titleiparta/index .html).
- National Endowment for the Arts—the largest annual funder of the arts in the United States. An independent federal agency, the National Endowment for the Arts is the official arts organization of the U.S. government. To apply for a grant, visit www.nea.gov/grants/apply/index.html.
- State and city organizations frequently fund special programs, such as the Education to Careers Program of the Chicago Public Schools and the New York State Universal Pre-K Program. Visit your state's department of education website and see what funding opportunities are available.

Business

The business world has been a source of funds for music programs, from large corporations such as the Ford Motor Company to smaller local companies. Some music directors solicit supplies from stores such as Wal-Mart, Target, and Home Depot. Music companies will sometimes donate instruments. Local chambers of commerce or clubs such as Kiwanis often provide monetary support also. A music program that actively performs for the local community often finds businesses and other community members who are happy to donate funds and support.

The MENC website maintains a list of grant money sources organized as federal, private, nonspecific, and region-specific, with links for each at www.menc .org/information/infoserv/Grants.html.

Performances themselves are opportunities to raise money, whether through ticket sales or simply informally passing the hat. At the same time, the music director can showcase the accomplishments and talents of students in the music program.

The fact that so many music educators actively engage in organizing and participating in fund-raising again emphasizes the hard work and dedication of these professionals. With a full teaching schedule, before- and after-school ensemble rehearsals, and performance schedules, music teachers frequently take on the role of funding various aspects of their music programs. We hope that showcasing the work of these music directors will provide ideas that will be helpful in your school or district.

SUMMARY
While no music program can be a perfect program, the submissions to MENC's Model Music Program show that music educators are full of ideas that are worth sharing with others in the profession. The many ideas shared in this chapter are the result of the hard work of music educators across the nation. One of them may be just the idea you've been looking for to ignite new interest in your program, get that community support you've been seeking, or direct the enthusiasm of your talented students.

Appendix A: Awardees

Adlai E. Stevenson High School
Lincolnshire, IL

Conners Emerson School
Bar Harbor, ME

East Meadow School District
Westbury, NY

East Ramapo Central School
  District
Spring Valley, NY

Haley Elementary School
Fort Wayne, IN

Nanuet Union Free School District
Nanuet, NY

Nora Davis Magnet School
Laurel, MS

Page Middle School
Page, AZ

Rutland City Public Schools
Rutland, VT

South Eastern School District
Fawn Grove, PA

The Spurwink School: Roosevelt
  Program
South Portland, ME

William Floyd School District
Mastic Beach, NY

Appendix B: All Submissions

INDIVIDUAL SCHOOLS AND GROUPS

A. E. Burdick School
Milwaukee, WI

Achieve Language Academy
St. Paul, MN

**Adlai E. Stevenson High School
Lincolnshire, IL

Alamo City School
Alamo, TN

All Saints Academy
Winter Haven, FL

Alma High School
Alma, AR

Arts Academy in the Woods
Warren, MI

Avondale West Elementary
Topeka, KS

Bartlett Music Academy
Bartlett, TN

Bassett High School
La Puente, CA

Bay High School
Bay Village, OH

Belle Chasse High School
Belle Chasse, LA

** = Programs selected as Model Music Programs
* = Programs receiving Honorable Mention

131

Bermudian Springs Elementary
   School
York Springs, PA

Blue Springs Elementary
Cleveland, TN

Bow-Dacious String Band
Urbana, IL

Brindlee Mountain High School
Guntersville, AL

Brittany Hill Middle School
Blue Springs, MO

Brownell-Talbot
Omaha, NE

Buckeye Valley East Elementary
Ashley, OH

Charleston County School of the
   Arts
North Charleston, SC

Chatham Central High School
Bear Creek, NC

Cheltenham Elementary
Cheltenham, PA

Churchland Elementary School
Portsmouth, VA

College Park UMC Primary
   School
Orlando, FL

Colvin Elementary
Wichita, KS

The Compass School
Kingston, RI

**Conners Emerson School
Bar Harbor, ME

The Cornerstone Christian School
Manchester, CT

Cortland City Schools/Smith
   Elementary School
Cortland, NY

"Crossroads of Music" at Orange
   Grove Elementary School
Whittier, CA

Crowley County High School
Ordway, CO

Delphi Community Schools
Delphi, IN

** = Programs selected as Model Music Programs
 * = Programs receiving Honorable Mention

Deltona Lakes Elementary
Deltona, FL

Denmark-Olar Elementary School
Denmark, SC

E. M. Daggett Middle School
Fort Worth, TX

East Central High School
St. Miles, IA

East Lincoln Middle School
Iron Station, NC

Eckstein Middle School
Seattle, WA

Egypt Lake Elementary
Tampa, FL

Emma E. Booker Elementary
Sarasota, FL

Far Hills Country Day School
Far Hills, NJ

Fingersteps Music
Edina, MN

Floyd Municipal Schools
Floyd, NM

Fremont Middle School
Pomona, CA

Gary Lighthouse Charter School
Gary, IN

George Washington Carver
    Elementary School
Lexington Park, MD

George Wythe High School
Wytheville, VA

Griffith Elementary
Phoenix, AZ

*Grissom Elementary School
Tulsa, OK

**Haley Elementary School
Fort Wayne, IN

Harlan Elementary School
Wilmington, DE

Hillrise Elementary School
Las Cruces, NM

Holgate Elementary School
Holgate, OH

Hoover Elementary School
Oakland, CA

** = Programs selected as Model Music Programs
* = Programs receiving Honorable Mention

Hunters Woods Elementary
  School
Reston, VA

Hyattsville Middle School
Hyattsville, MD

Inman Middle School
Paris, TN

Jefferson Township Jr./Sr. High
  School
Dayton, OH

John F. Kennedy Catholic High
  School
Somers, NY

John Marshall High School
Los Angeles, CA

John Q. Adams Middle School
Metairie, LA

Jones College Prep High School
Chicago, IL

Kent Elementary School
Kent, WA

Knowlton Township Elementary
  School
Delaware, NJ

Krejci Academy
Naperville, IL

Lake Zurich High School
Lake Zurich, IL

Lexington School
Lexington, AL

Madison High School
Rexburg, ID

Magnolia Middle School
Joppa, MD

Marimor School
Lima, OH

Metamora Township High
  School
Metamora, IL

Middletown High School
Middletown, NY

Monroe Clark Middle School
San Diego, CA

Myrtle Place Elementary School
Lafayette, LA

Neal Middle School
Durham, NC

** = Programs selected as Model Music Programs
 * = Programs receiving Honorable Mention

New York Mills Public School
New York Mills, MN

The New York Pops
New York City, NY

**Nora Davis Magnet School
Laurel, MS

Nordhoff High School
Ojai, CA

North Port High School
North Port, FL

Northside Elementary School
Warner Robins, GA

Odyssey Elementary School
Everett, WA

Oliver Wendell Holmes
Dallas, TX

Osage City High School
Osage City, KS

**Page Middle School
Page, AZ

Piano Play Music Systems
Sherman Oaks, CA

Plant City High School
Plant City, FL

Plymouth Elementary School
Plymouth Meeting, PA

Pocahontas Middle School
Powhatan, VA

Renaissance Arts Academy
Los Angeles, CA

Rib Mountain Elementary School
Wausau, WI

Roopville Elementary School
Roopville, GA

Rosemount Middle School
Rosemount, MN

Ruby Shaw Elementary School
Mesquite, TX

Saint Matthew School
Indianapolis, IN

*Sandstone Middle School
Hermiston, OR

Seaford Middle School
Seaford, DE

** = Programs selected as Model Music Programs
* = Programs receiving Honorable Mention

Servite High School
Anaheim, CA

Shaler Area Middle School
Glenshaw, PA

Six to Six Interdistrict Magnet
   School
Bridgeport, CT

South Central Middle School
Emerson, GA

Southside Christian School
Simpsonville, SC

Spring Hills School
Roselle, IL

The Spurwink School: Cummings
   Program
Portland, ME

**The Spurwink School: Roosevelt
   Program
South Portland, ME

Stoneleigh Elementary School
Baltimore, MD

Tekamah-Herman Public Schools
Tekamah, NE

Thoreau Elementary School
Madison, WI

Timber Grove Elementary School
Owings Mills, MD

Tohatchi High School
Tohatchi, NM

Tom Joy Elementary School
Nashville, TN

Union County High School
Maynardville, TN

W. R. Odell Elementary School
Concord, NC

Wantagh High School
Wantagh, NY

Washington Youth Choir
Washington, DC

Waveland Elementary School
Waveland, IN

Waverly High School
Waverly, OH

Waverly Jr. High School
Waverly, OH

** = Programs selected as Model Music Programs
 * = Programs receiving Honorable Mention

Wea Ridge Middle School
Lafayette, IN

Wheeling Middle School
Wheeling, WV

Whitehorse High School
Montezuma Creek, UT

Woodside School
Woodside, CA

DISTRICTS

Arrowhead Area Consortium
   Bands
Hartland, WI

Atlanta Public Schools
Atlanta, GA

Broomfield Orchestra Program of
   the Boulder Valley Schools
Broomfield, CO

Cache County School District
Logan, UT

Caldwell School District 132
Caldwell, ID

Clark County School District
Las Vegas, NV

**East Meadow School District
Westbury, NY

**East Ramapo Central School
   District
Spring Valley, NY

Indian Prairie School District 204
Naperville, IL

Johnson City Central School District
Johnson City, NY

Liberty/Victory Charter Public
   Charter Schools
Nampa, ID

Lincoln Unified School District
Stockton, CA

Martin County Schools
Inez, KY

**Nanuet Union Free School District
Nanuet, NY

Paramus Public Schools
Paramus, NJ

Rochester City School District
Rochester, NY

**Rutland City Public Schools
Rutland, VT

** = Programs selected as Model Music Programs
* = Programs receiving Honorable Mention

**South Eastern School District
Fawn Grove, PA

Stanhope Public Schools
Stanhope, NJ

Tulsa Public Schools
Tulsa, OK

Westside Community Schools
District 66
Omaha, NE

Wicomico County Public Schools
Salisbury, MD

**William Floyd School District
Mastic Beach, NY

** = Programs selected as Model Music Programs
 * = Programs receiving Honorable Mention

References

Brown, T. J. 2000. Music education for the deaf and hearing-handicapped. *The Colorado Music Educator* 47(3):26–28.

Campbell, Patricia Shehan. 1996. *Music in cultural context: Eight views on world music education.* Reston, Va.: MENC.

Choksy, Lois. 1974. *The Kodály method: Comprehensive music education from infant to adult.* Englewood Cliffs, N.J.: Prentice Hall. Also available at www.musicforlittlepeople.co.uk/ZKodaly.asp.

Consortium of National Arts Education Associations. 1994. *National Standards for Arts Education.* Reston, Va.: MENC.

Lehman, Paul. 2000. Introduction. In B. Reimer, ed., *Performing with understanding: The challenge of the National Standards for Music Education,* 3–6. Reston, Va.: MENC.

McCoy, Peter. 2003. Digital technologies in the music classroom. In *Spotlight on technology in the music classroom: Selected articles from state MEA journals,* 110–12. Reston, Va.: MENC.

National Center on Education and the Economy. 2006. *Tough choices or tough times: The Report of the New Commission on the Skills of the American Workforce.* Hoboken, N.J.: Jossey-Bass.

U.S. Office of Indian Education Programs. n.d. *Johnson-O'Malley Program handbook.* www.oiep.bia.edu/jomdocs/ JOMHANDBOOK%20REV.011403.doc (accessed March 23, 2007).

Membership Invitation

MENC: The National Association for Music Education
invites you enjoy the benefits of membership in
the only professional association dedicated to music for all!

Are you a music teacher?
A music education student?
A parent? A caregiver? Retired? Collegiate? Corporate?
Or simply a friend of music?

There's a place for *everyone* in music education.

MENC: The Largest Arts Education Association on Earth.

Come see where you belong: www.menc.org

1-800-828-0229 (outside the U.S., call 703-860-4000)

Music. Learn it. Live it. Love it. For life.*